performance

Fly Casting

0 11557 00734 3

performance

Fly Casting
an illustrated guide

jon b. cave

illustrations by
joe mahler

HEADWATER
BOOKS

STACKPOLE
BOOKS

Published by
STACKPOLE BOOKS
5067 Ritter Road
Mechanicsburg, PA 17055
www.stackpolebooks.com

Printed in the United States

First edition

Cover design by Caroline M. Stover

10 9 8 7 6 5 4 3 2 1

Library of Congress Cataloging-in-Publication Data
Cave, Jon B., 1946–.
   Performance fly casting / Jon B. Cave.
        p. cm.
   Includes index.
   ISBN-13: 978-0-8117-0734-3 (pbk.)
   ISBN-10: 0-8117-0734-2 (pbk.)
   1. Fly casting. I. Title.
SH454.2.C38 2011
799.12′4—dc22

                                        2010052889

To Poots, the bravest person I know.

contents

acknowledgments

I'M EXTREMELY GRATEFUL to the individuals who helped bring *Performance Fly Casting* to fruition, and in recognition of their generous assistance, I extend a heartfelt thanks.

The idea for this book wasn't mine. My brother and lifelong fishing companion, Paul, repeatedly encouraged me to do it after years of my writing a regular casting column for *Fly Fishing in Salt Waters* magazine. He also patiently took hundreds of photos that served as excellent references for the illustrations.

I couldn't have asked for a better fly-casting illustrator than Joe Mahler. Relying on a combination of his artistic eye and fly-fishing experience, Joe captured in detail the very essence of the casting stroke.

Jay Nichols, Judith Schnell, Amy Lerner, and the staff at Stackpole Books deserve a great deal of credit for their hard work in taking on this project and making my vision become a reality.

My deep appreciation goes to fly-fishing enthusiast Ruth Stokes and casting aficionado Dave Johnson for offering their valuable opinions and suggestions.

Thanks also to Marc Bale at Sage Rods, John Harder at Rio Products, and Raz Reid for ensuring that I've always had the finest fly rods and lines.

Last, although most assuredly not least, I wish to express gratitude to the late guide/tournament caster/instructor Ed Mueller who generously served as my earliest mentor.

introduction

HAVING THE CONFIDENCE and skill to instinctively make a perfect cast to a wary fish under difficult circumstances is the pinnacle of fly fishing. But fly casting should also be easy and effortless, whether you're making a short presentation or one in excess of 100 feet. That level of performance requires fundamentally sound technique that will serve as the foundation for understanding and mastering many types of casts, such as a standard pick-up-and-lay-down (overhead), sidearm, curve, Belgian, serpentine, roll, speed, stacked-leader, tuck, or mend.

There are many viable casting styles, but some are more versatile than others. When deciding which style to choose, consider whether it is easy to learn and can be adapted to a variety of situations in both fresh and salt water.

As a fly-fishing guide, author, and founder of the longest established fly-fishing school in the South, I have the opportunity to share the exciting world of fly fishing with many anglers in my home state of Florida as well as in various national and international locations. Drawing from those experiences, I wrote *Performance Fly Casting* with the following objectives in mind:

- Create a practical and uncomplicated casting book that is comprehensive enough to increase the casting performance of fly fishers at all skill levels.
- Let the text stand alone so that it is easily understood without photos or drawings. That way the illustrations will support the text instead of the other way around.

- Follow the methods I use to successfully teach students at my casting schools and seminars.
- Present the text in a logical sequence that is easy to follow.
- Focus primarily on the pick-up-and-lay-down or overhead cast, because it serves as the basis for almost all other casts.
- Discuss potential casting problems and their solutions.

Some fundamental elements pertain to the execution of *all* efficient casting strokes, and it is the degree to which these fundamentals are mastered that distinguishes casters with the highest level of expertise from those at lesser skill levels. Consequently, when carefully reading this book and studying the illustrations, it is imperative that you focus primarily on the fundamentals while at the same time paying close attention to the less obvious details and nuances that also have a significant impact on perfecting your casting skills. Although the chapters are meant to be read in numeric order, less accomplished casters and beginners should spend additional time going over Chapter 9, The Ground Stroke.

In trying to either learn or improve casting technique, it's often just as important to know what's wrong with a cast as it is to know what's right. Since you can't correct problems that you don't recognize, *Performance Casting* includes details of common casting mistakes, along with their solutions. When referring to Joe Mahler's illustrations, please note that all casting miscues are marked with a thumbs-down.

Using the comprehensive methodology clearly detailed within this book in the form of text and illustrations, you can develop the kind of instinctive feel and effective technique necessary to take your casting skills to the next level, whether you're new to fly fishing or an experienced hand. Developing a smooth and relaxed delivery, throwing tighter loops, achieving greater distance effortlessly, casting under windy conditions, eliminating slack, increasing accuracy, making better presentations, and double hauling efficiently—all of this is what makes up performance fly casting! Let's get started.

—Jon Cave
Black Hammock, Florida
September 2010

one

Equipment

QUALITY EQUIPMENT, especially the line, rod, and leader, plays a critical role in improving fly-casting performance. While you do not need to take out a second mortgage on a fly-fishing outfit in order to attain a high skill level, you should buy the best gear that you can afford. As with most things purchased in life, you basically get what you pay for.

Prior to making a purchase, gather information about an item before heading to the fly shop. It's certainly OK to consult with friends, fly-shop personnel, magazines, and books, but avoid relying on them entirely. Selecting a top-notch fly-fishing outfit is highly subjective, and opinions will vary from one fly fisher to another as to what is ideal, so the final decision needs to be yours alone. This chapter will help you evaluate lines, rods, reels, backing, and leaders in order to make the selection process easier.

Fly Lines

The fly line can have a more significant impact on casting performance than any other piece of equipment, but all too often it isn't given the attention it deserves. Since some lines work better than others with a specific rod or under a given set of circumstances, all serious casters should thoroughly understand the effects that line weight, taper, density, and maintenance have on casting.

FLY-LINE WEIGHTS

Fly fishers rely on the mass of a weighted line to load the rod and carry a comparatively weightless fly to a fish. The larger, heavier, and more wind-resistant the fly, the greater the mass or weight of the line should be.

In the early 1960s, the American Fishing Tackle Manufacturers Association (AFTMA) introduced a standardized method for measuring fly-line weights. Lines were categorized using a numbering system that ranged from 1 through 15; the higher the number, the heavier the line. (Some highly specialized lines fall outside this range, including 0-, 00-, 000-, and 16-weights.) According to AFTMA standards, designations are based on the weight in grains of the first 30 feet of line, excluding the level tip section. For instance, the forward 30-foot section of all 8-weight lines weighs approximately 210 grains.

This same system prevails today, although it has been bastardized to some degree. Many lines are now manufactured slightly heavier than the AFTMA tolerance levels allow so that they are easier to cast with modern powerful rods. For that same reason, a few lines are now being labeled strictly by grain weight (e.g., 250 grains) instead of the designated AFTMA number.

To help reduce any confusion, individuals not yet familiar with weight guidelines should consider using light lines in the 3- to 6-weight range for casting small flies to trout

Line Weight Designations in Grains

Weight	Grains	Tolerance Range
1-weight	60	54–66
2-weight	80	74–86
3-weight	100	94–106
4-weight	120	114–126
5-weight	140	134–146
6-weight	160	152–168
7-weight	185	177–193
8-weight	210	202–218
9-weight	240	230–250
10-weight	280	270–290
11-weight	330	318–342
12-weight	380	368–392
13-weight	450	
14-weight	500	
15-weight	550	

and panfish; 7- and 8-weights for bass; 7- through 9-weights for shallow saltwater flats; 10- through 12-weights for deep flats and nearshore fishing; and 12-weight or heavier for casting to offshore pelagics. This list certainly isn't all encompassing, but it offers a good starting point for each type of fishing.

FLY-LINE TAPERS

Taper refers to the contour or shape of a line from front to back. Unfortunately, so many different fly-line tapers are available today that their sheer numbers alone can be intimidating and confusing when the time comes to choose the most appropriate one. It seems that almost every conceivable angling situation and each species of gamefish has its own designated line, and a few even bear the names of some well-known fly fishers. Bass taper, saltwater taper, trout taper, distance taper, and general-purpose taper are only a few of the choices. But despite the ostensibly endless number of tapers available today, all of them are variations of three basic configurations: weight-forward (WF), double-taper (DT), and level (L) lines. Level lines have no taper. Although very inexpensive, they have only limited application and lack the versatility of other lines, so they are not described in detail in this section. Another system that fly fishers occasionally use is the shooting taper (head), a variant of the weight-forward.

Weight-Forward Tapers

Because of their versatility, weight-forward tapers are the most popular. In the hands of a competent caster, they have the potential for making the longest casts without affecting the quality of the presentation. Weight-forward lines have a relatively complex construction consisting of two sections integrated into a single piece. The heavy front "head" section is connected to a thin, level "running line." By modifying the head and, to a much lesser degree, the running line, manufacturers can create a variety of weight-forward lines designed to perform optimally under different circumstances.

To further understand the dynamics of a weight-forward taper, you must be familiar with each of the head's integrated segments—the tip, front taper, belly, and rear taper—as well as the overall head length. By varying the lengths and diameters of each of these segments, fly-line companies can design lines with unique casting characteristics.

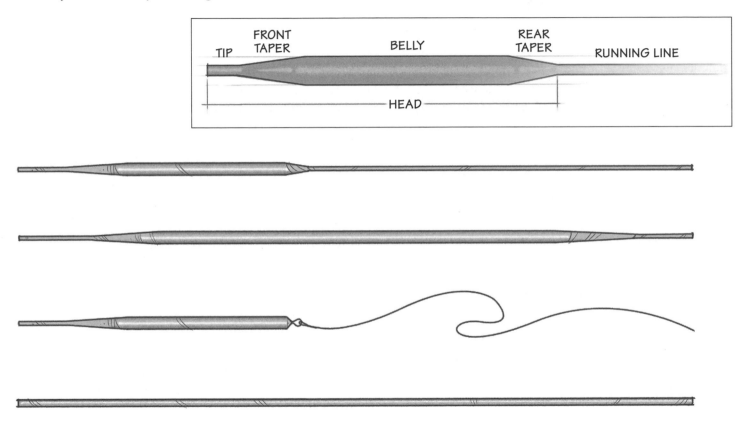

Line tapers (top to bottom): weight-forward, double taper, shooting head with running line attached, level.

Tip

The tip of a weight-forward line is a level section up to 12 inches long to which the leader system is attached. Its length allows for cutting off and reattaching the leader system several times without significantly affecting the shape and performance of the front taper. Tip diameter also has a bearing on how a line unrolls. A line with a small-diameter tip allows you to make a more delicate presentation, whereas a thick tip enables a more powerful delivery.

Front Taper

The length of the front taper, in combination with the diameter of the tip, determines the manner in which the fly is delivered and how the casting energy dissipates as the line unrolls during a cast. A line that incorporates a lengthy front taper with a small-diameter tip will dissipate the energy of a cast earlier and more significantly than one that combines a short front taper with a thick tip. Therefore, all other things being equal, longer front tapers are a good choice for relatively small flies or when a quiet presentation is required. On the other hand, a comparatively short front taper has a more powerful turnover that makes it easier to cast large or heavy flies even when it's windy. However, one of the shortcomings of extremely blunt tapers is that they have a tendency to "hook," "kick," or "tuck" at the end of the cast. Some may also land too harshly for spooky fish.

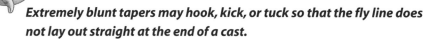

Extremely blunt tapers may hook, kick, or tuck so that the fly line does not lay out straight at the end of a cast.

Belly

The belly section is situated between the front and rear tapers. Because the belly is the thickest part of the head, it holds most of the energy in a cast; this energy is then dissipated through the forward taper and tip. A long belly, with its inherent delayed turnover and enhanced control, is ideal for making long, accurate casts, whereas a short belly is better suited to short, quick presentations.

Rear Taper

The rear taper is the transitional area between the belly and the thin-diameter running line. The length of the rear taper affects a caster's control over the entire head and thus the smoothness with which the line can be cast. A long rear taper provides the most control and therefore has the potential for casting the smoothest line, whereas a short rear taper is often the best choice when presentations must be made quickly.

Head Length

The length of the head has a great deal of influence on casting distance and the number of false casts needed to make a presentation. Depending on its design, the head can vary anywhere between 30 and 65 feet long. Because a lengthy head takes more time to unroll than a shorter one, the longest heads have the potential of achieving the greatest distance, but there are trade-offs. Longer heads may require more false casting to reach a given distance, and they can be harder to aerialize than short versions. Consequently, even under identical circumstances, not all casters will benefit equally from the same head design. Top-notch casters can reach extreme distances with a minimal number of false casts whether the head is long or short. On the other hand, the average caster may benefit more from short- to medium-length heads because there is less line to manage outside the rod tip during false casting.

There are several ways to check the taper on the fly line you currently own or may be considering. Years ago, many fly fishers used a micrometer to check tapers, and although that is still a viable alternative, there are simpler methods. Today most line manufacturers have catalogs or tear sheets available that show the head dimensions and tapers on their various lines. That same information can usually be obtained on their websites as well. In addition, some fly-line boxes have diagrams of the individual head configurations. The information gleaned from one of these resources will reveal any differences in head design so that you'll be better able to select the taper that best suits your needs.

Many individuals are so confused by the number of different weight-forward tapers on the market that they simply succumb to the labeling on the box: "I'm going fly-fishing for bonefish so I guess I need a bonefish taper." Although that line may perform well for the average caster under a specific set of circumstances, another line, or maybe several other lines, might perform the task just as well or even better. For example, a bonefish line may work equally well for redfish and permit.

Relying simply on the label (e.g., bonefish taper, trout taper, bass taper, and so on) can lead to other problems as well. For example, you will find a wide array of bonefish tapers available from the different line manufacturers and even within the same company—each with its own uniquely tapered head. Since line designs are not standardized by name, a look at the head dimensions and taper will reveal which of the bonefish lines is best for the occasion. Contrarily, lines with different names may have the same taper. For instance, some saltwater, bonefish, and bass lines are practically identical except for some rather minor distin-

guishing features that have nothing to do with their taper, and these lines can be used interchangeably in many instances.

When choosing a weight-forward line, you will have to make some compromises, as no taper is perfect in all situations. Moreover, fly fishers often get so caught up in using specialty tapers that they overlook the fact that a standard, general-purpose weight-forward line can deliver good all-around performance under a wide variety of conditions.

Double-Tapers

Double-taper lines are level throughout the middle and tapered symmetrically at each end. The thick center section makes them a good choice in scenarios that call for frequent roll casts and mends, and the long front taper delivers a relatively gentle presentation that is very effective for skittish fish. They are especially popular with trout anglers. Since both ends are identical, another supposed advantage is that the line can be reversed after the presentation end wears out; however, by the time one end is worn out, the entire line is often unusable as well. They are not recommended for saltwater use, because their relatively large diameter takes up valuable reel space that is better reserved for additional backing to fight powerful marine fish. In addition, a double-taper is a poor choice for making long casts, because its thickness doesn't allow the line to shoot as easily through the guides as the thin running line on a weight-forward taper.

Shooting Heads

In addition to weight-forward, double-taper, and level line configurations, many fly fishers occasionally use a shooting taper system. Similar to a weight-forward line, a shooting taper system consists of two components: the running line and the head. The head portion is usually about 30 to 40 feet long and has a taper that somewhat resembles that of a weight-forward line, except there is little or no rear taper. The running or shooting line has a very small diameter that allows for great shootability. Shooting taper systems are designed more to produce long casts than they are for making good presentations, and as such, they should not be used as a substitute for standard lines.

There are two types of shooting taper systems: interchangeable and integrated. In an interchangeable system, the head and running line are separate components that are attached via either a loop-to-loop or other knot connection, thus giving you the option to switch from one head to another with relative ease. The integrated system combines the head and running line into one seamless piece. Whether you prefer an integrated or nonintegrated shooting taper system, this is one instance when it's always a good idea to upline the rod by at least one line weight for optimal loading.

FLY-LINE DENSITIES

In addition to taper, you must also consider the density or buoyancy factor of the fly line. Density variations and their alphabetic designations are as follows: floating (F), full-sinking (S), sinking-tip (F/S), and intermediate (I). Keeping different densities of line at hand allows you to fish at various depths and provides opportunities to adapt to other conditions as well.

Because of its versatility and good castability, a floating line is usually the mainstay of any angler's fly-line arsenal. Both surface and subsurface flies can be fished effectively with a floating line, and it is the best line to use during practice sessions. Moreover, the buoyancy of a floating line makes it far and away the easiest line to lift or pick up off the water when you're initiating a backcast.

Lines that sink, including full-sinking and sinking-tip versions, are available with rates of descent that range from a relatively slow 1 inch per second to a quick 9 inches per second. To complicate matters even more, a few sinking lines give the grain weight of the line on the label instead of the AFTMA numerical designation. It is important to note, as described in the fly-line weights section, that the grain weight is simply a reference to be used in selecting a line that will appropriately load a fly rod. It is *not* an indicator of a line's sink rate.

Intermediate lines are sometimes referred to as having a neutral density, and a common belief is that they neither float nor sink, but stay suspended just below the water surface. In actuality, however, they have a slightly negative density, which causes them to continuously sink, albeit at a slow rate. They are particularly useful for fishing just below the surface or for working a fly over submerged structure. An intermediate line is also a good choice on breezy days when the wind would otherwise blow a floating line across the surface, thereby creating unwanted drag.

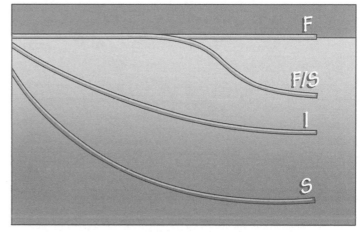

Fly line densities (top to bottom): floating, sinking-tip, intermediate, and sinking.

There are other density characteristics worth noting. The higher the density, and therefore the faster the sink rate, the smaller the diameter of the line will be. For example, a floating line is thicker than a sinking line with the equivalent AFTMA designation. That's because the material that makes a line buoyant also increases its thickness.

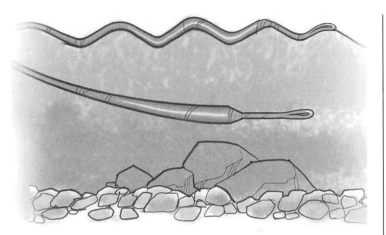

An intermediate line is a good choice in breezy conditions because it is less susceptible to wave action and surface wind than a floating line.

You can take advantage of the differences in thickness by opting for some variation of a sinking line on windy days if the water is sufficiently deep to prevent the line and fly from hanging up on the bottom. The sinking line's small diameter provides better penetration into the wind when cast than would a fatter floating line. A thinner line is also advantageous in the open sea, where a line-sizzling run by a huge pelagic fish would otherwise create a large belly in a floating line.

Complications related to density and diameter often arise when casting sinking-tip lines. The consolidation of a thick floating section with a thinner sinking section creates

a hinge point where the two segments are conjoined. The hinge prevents the casting loop from unrolling, or turning over, smoothly. This problem is most acute with the thinnest high-density tips but is far less pronounced with thicker slow-sinking and intermediate tips.

FLY-LINE COLOR

Fly-line color could affect casting results. Bright-colored lines are the easiest to keep track of in the water after you have made the presentation, and you can also readily monitor them in your peripheral vision during a cast. However,

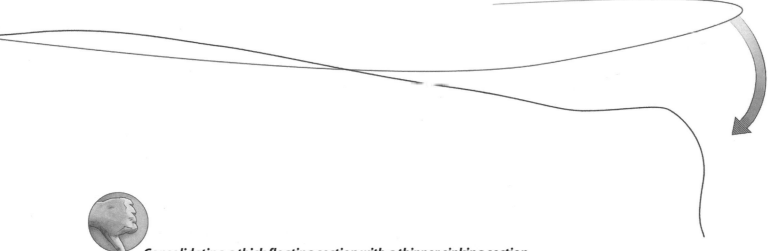

Consolidating a thick floating section with a thinner sinking section to form a sinking-tip line creates a hinge point that may prevent the loop from unrolling smoothly.

there are two schools of thought with regard to color. One believes that a colorful line may frighten fish. The other maintains that if the cast is properly executed, the line should never enter a fish's field of view, even though a line's shadow may occasionally scare fish. There's something to be said for both opinions. Ideally, the line shouldn't be close enough for a fish to see, but circumstances aren't always perfect, and an occasional glimpse by fish is always a possibility, particularly in close quarters and in clear water. In addition, some fish may be more easily frightened than others. Nevertheless, as far as I'm concerned, the benefits of a colorful line outweigh any disadvantages in most circumstances.

FLY-LINE CORE MATERIALS

The vast majority of manufacturers use either monofilament or some type of braided nylon as the core material for their fly lines. Lines with a braided nylon core are preferred for cool-water environments, as they often turn limp and become difficult to use in the warmest temperatures. Conversely, lines that have a monofilament core are a better choice in hot climates, and as a result, they are commonly used to make tropical saltwater lines. But as temperatures cool, some types of mono coil up like a Slinky toy, and they can be exceedingly frustrating to cast under these conditions.

MAINTENANCE

A fly line's condition substantially affects casting performance. A line that is properly maintained will cast, shoot, and float much better than one that becomes dirty, cracked, dried out, or otherwise damaged. Because a clean, lubricated, and supple line performs better than a neglected one, casting problems can be reduced as well.

Regardless of how clean a body of water may appear, algae, dirt, and salt (in marine environments) will adhere to a fly line during the course of a day's fishing. In order to keep a line in top working order, it should be cleaned after each use. Begin by washing the line with a mild soap solution, then rinse and dry. If necessary, apply a line dressing recommended by the manufacturer, allow the dressing sufficient time to penetrate the finish, and polish with a soft cloth. If the dirty line resists the normal cleaning routine, buff it with a specialized ultrafine abrasive pad available through most fly-line companies. Avoid using detergents or automotive vinyl protectants, as they can dry out a line over time and eventually cause it to crack. Heat, insect repellent, sun lotion, and prolonged exposure to the sun can also cause damage.

Line twist is another problem that affects casting efficiency. Kicking line while it's lying on the deck of a boat or on the ground can cause it to twist. Likewise, failing to cast all of the line pulled from the reel will create twists. Casting with nonaerodynamic flies such as poppers can spin the line as well. To eliminate the candy-cane-like twists, remove the fly and either troll the line behind a boat or cast downcurrent and allow sufficient time for it to unwind.

Coils in the line are the result of a line's inelasticity or "memory." They frequently develop when the line has been stored on the reel for a lengthy period and are especially common in cool temperatures. Lines with stiff monofilament cores, such as those designed for tropical heat, have a tendency to coil as well. In the most severe cases, the line takes on the appearance of a mattress coil spring. Coils are routinely removed by stretching the entire line.

Unless a line has a welded loop at the tip, the knot connecting the leader system to the fly line should be inspected on a regular basis to make sure that no cracks develop immediately behind the connection. Any such cracks allow water to be absorbed into the line's core, thereby causing the tip to sink. The submerged tip can negatively affect the pickup as well as the presentation. The problem is easily resolved by cutting away the faulty connection and replacing it with another.

Fly Rods

Selecting a quality fly rod and correctly matching it to the specific line weight you've chosen is the next step in assembling a fly-fishing outfit that is capable of high-performance casting. For instance, an 8-weight line requires an 8-weight rod. Most fly rods can readily handle a line that is either one weight heavier or lighter than the one designated, but top performance is almost always derived from using the line weight marked on the rod. Although a manufacturer may occasionally under- or overrate the recommended line weight of a rod, the vast majority are very accurate in their evaluations.

As a matter of course, some fly fishers consistently advocate uplining any rod by one or more weights in order to better feel the rod load, but that is often a makeshift

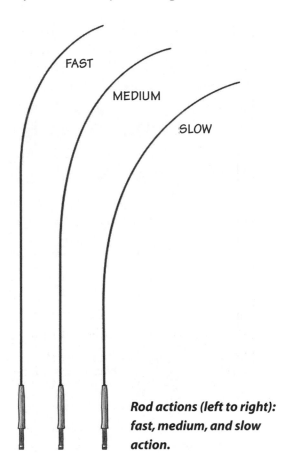

Rod actions (left to right): fast, medium, and slow action.

FAST

MEDIUM

SLOW

solution to poor casting technique. Actually, the additional weight that comes from uplining softens the action of a rod and makes it more flexible. Wider loops are usually an unintended result. Furthermore, when aerializing (false-casting) a long length of line, the added weight may soften the rod to such a degree that the rod butt is no longer strong enough to satisfactorily support the additional line, which becomes difficult to manage. By comparison, using the recommended line keeps the rod action as the designer intended, which usually results in tighter loops and the ability to false-cast more line with fewer problems. Although some circumstances call for uplining, they usually involve shooting tapers or situations where casts are consistently less than 30 feet—the amount of line used to measure its AFTMA weight. That's because in those instances there isn't enough line to load the rod adequately in the first place, and uplining provides the additional necessary weight.

Although a fly rod is supposed to *sufficiently* load with the weight of 30 feet of line outside the tip, each rod has a "sweet spot" at which it is *optimally* loaded—usually with a length of line in excess of 30 feet. That length will be different for each line taper and density. The sweet spot will also vary from one caster to another. Wind conditions have an effect too. The sweet spot is a highly subjective feel to which casters become sensitive over a period of time, rather than anything that can be objectively described or measured.

There are three basic fly-rod actions: fast, medium, and slow. When loaded under the weight of a fly line, fast rods are designed to bend primarily in the upper 25 percent, medium-action rods bend toward the middle, and slow-action rods bend in a parabolic arc throughout their length. Progressive-action rods load increasingly, or progressively, farther down the blank as more line, and therefore more weight, is added to the cast.

Fast-action rods have the potential to generate excellent line speed and form the tightest loops. Because they flex primarily at the tip, fast rods load quicker than those with medium or slow actions. They also have a comparatively powerful butt section that makes them a good choice for fighting big fish, presenting large flies, and casting under windy conditions.

Slow-action rods bend throughout their length under the weight of the line. They require an easy and more deliberate casting stroke than rods with faster actions. The full flex of a slow-action rod also acts as a large shock absorber when fighting fish and thus provides superior protection for light tippets.

Medium-action rods are a compromise between those with fast and slow actions. As such, they possess many similar good qualities of each, albeit to a lesser degree. Casting ease, protecting light tippets, forming tight loops, and developing good line speed are all attributes of medium-action rods. They are a good choice for individuals who need a rod that will perform well under a wide variety of conditions.

Another factor to consider is flexibility. In comparing different fly rods of the same line weight and action, some will be more flexible than others. Consequently, when an equal length of fly line is cast with each rod, the most limber models will load more readily and bend deeper than stiffer ones. For example, Brands A and B are both 8-weight fly rods with fast actions. But if Brand A is more flexible, it will load easier and bend deeper under a given length of fly line than Brand B.

The dampening capability of a fly rod is its most important characteristic. Rods that vibrate significantly at the completion of either the backcast or forward cast will form inefficient, wavy loops, whereas rods that dampen quickly, with almost no oscillation, have the most potential

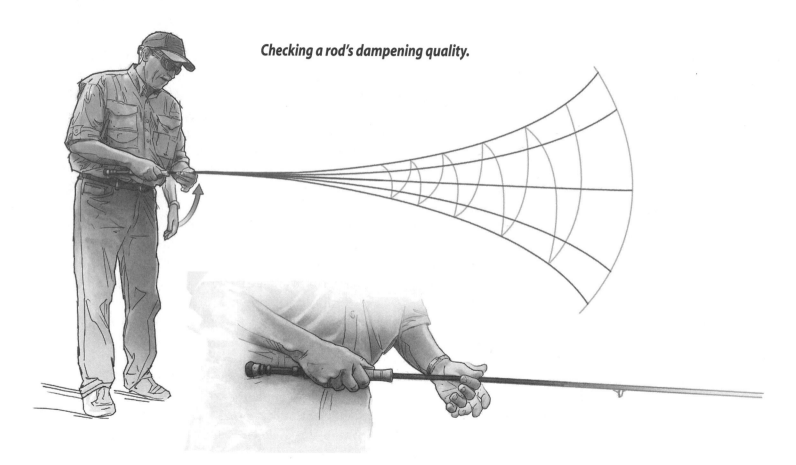

Checking a rod's dampening quality.

to throw a smooth, ripple-free line. To test for dampening, hold a rod loosely by the cork grip and shake the tip slightly so that it oscillates. With the opposite hand, grab the blank about a foot above the cork, and then quickly release it. The best rods will dampen immediately, but significant vibration will be detected in those of lesser quality.

A rod's length, guides, and grip also affect casting. To a great extent, long rods have the ability to cast farther than shorter ones. In addition, large-diameter guides reduce friction and allow line to shoot more easily than with smaller guides. When it comes to a grip, cork has a feel that no synthetic material can duplicate, but the shape and diameter of the grip are important as well. Small-diameter grips may feel comfortable initially, but they often cause cramping and muscle fatigue over prolonged periods. Comparatively thicker grips that are ergonomically shaped provide the most long-term comfort.

Fly Reels

A fly reel can't improve casting performance, but the wrong one can have a marginally negative impact. For the most comfortable casting, there should be a relatively even balance between the tip and the butt when you hold the fly-fishing outfit. An overly heavy reel matched to one of latest ultralightweight rods can make the whole outfit seem ponderous and bottom-heavy. Likewise, a reel with an extremely small diameter will produce tight, Slinky toy coils in the line, which will prevent it from sliding smoothly through the guides. Durability, drag, and handing are other parameters that figure into the purchasing process, but these features are unrelated to fly casting and thus are not covered here.

Backing

In choosing backing, the leader's tippet strength is the primary consideration. The breaking strength of the backing should always exceed the breaking strength of the tippet, so that in the event of a break-off, the line will separate at the tippet instead of the backing, thereby saving the loss of an entire fly line. For subduing big fish with heavy tackle (usually 10-weight and heavier) and leaders up to 20-pound-test, 30-pound-test Dacron line is best for backing, whereas

20-pound-test line is a better choice for lighter gear with finer tippets.

Some fly fishers use braided or fused polyethylene gel (also called gel-spun) line as backing, because it has a significantly smaller diameter than Dacron line of the same strength. The smaller diameter allows for much greater line capacity on a reel (over 50 percent more than with Dacron) and creates less drag in the water when a fish makes a long run into the backing. These traits make gel-spun line highly popular with offshore fly fishers, where extra backing and reduced water drag are distinct advantages in battling large oceanic species capable of making runs of up to several hundred yards. The extra backing also increases the effective diameter of the arbor for quicker line pickup. Nevertheless, gel-spun line has its disadvantages. It costs almost double the price of Dacron for an equivalent length, and you'll also have to purchase more gel-spun to fill a reel; it occasionally digs into itself on the spool and causes snarling; and it can be difficult to tie knots with. I prefer Dacron for everything except offshore fly fishing. If you decide to use gel-spun line for backing, substitute 30- to 35-pound-test gel-spun for 20-pound-test Dacron, and 50- to 65-pound-test gel-spun for 30-pound-test Dacron.

Unless you can make casts longer than the length of fly line, backing has no effect on the cast. For those who cast farther than the entire length of the fly line (and it is my hope that you will be able to after using the techniques in this book), I recommend attaching about a 20-foot section of Cortland or Gudebrod finely braided monofilament running line (30- to 35-pound-test works best) between the rear end of the fly line and the backing. The braided mono will shoot significantly better and tangle far less than soft, thin backing.

Leaders

The leader is an almost invisible length of monofilament that connects the fly line to the fly and is arguably just as important to casting performance as the fly line and rod. As the loop unrolls, the leader should smoothly transfer energy from the fly line to the fly so that it has enough momentum to turn over at the end of a cast. However, in some instances the fly-and-leader combination may not unroll sufficiently. When that situation occurs, some fly fishers might assume that the problem results from a casting malfunction, when in fact the leader may be the cause. In choosing a suitable leader, consider the following: tapered leaders cast better than a level piece of monofilament; and the larger and more wind-resistant the fly, the heavier the leader should be, and vice versa. There are three basic leader types: tapered, big-game, and level.

TAPERED LEADERS

Tapered leaders come in both knotted and knotless variations. A knotless leader is a single piece of monofilament that has been extruded through a machine to a desired taper. In contrast, knotted versions are constructed of various thicknesses and lengths of monofilament tied together to form a single tapered unit. Both leader styles are normally described by their length and tippet size, such as a 10-foot, 2X leader.

When selecting a suitable length, keep in mind that the more subtle the presentation must be, the longer the leader necessary to achieve the desired result. As examples, a leader might have to be as long as 14 feet for a spooky and selective brown trout in a quiet pool, whereas a relatively short 8-foot leader would be more appropriate for an aggressive largemouth bass in heavy cover.

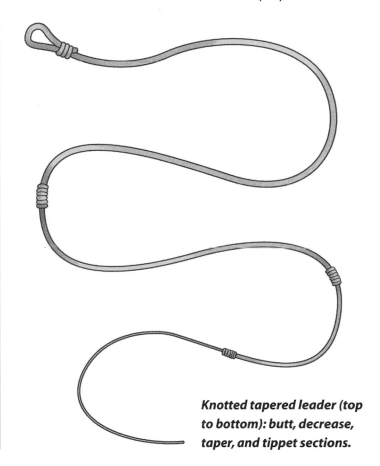

Knotted tapered leader (top to bottom): butt, decrease, taper, and tippet sections.

Tippet X Values, Diameters, and Breaking Strengths

X Value	Diameter (inches)	Breaking Strength Range*
04X	.015	15–26 pound-test
03X	.014	13–22 pound-test
02X	.013	12–20 pound-test
01X	.012	10–18.5 pound-test
0X	.011	8–15.5 pound-test
1X	.010	6.5–13.5 pound-test
2X	.009	6–12 pound-test
3X	.008	6–8.8 pound-test
4X	.007	4–7 pound-test
5X	.006	4–5.2 pound-test
6X	.005	2–3.8 pound-test
7X	.004	2–2.7 pound-test
8X	.003	1–1.8 pound-test

*Ranges are approximate and based on popular tippet brands.

The tippet is the thinnest, weakest, and forward-most section (15 inches or longer when attached to a fly) of a tapered leader. If the tippet diameter is too small for the fly, the leader will not completely unroll and may even collapse into a pile in the most extreme cases. On the other hand, a tippet that is too large cannot dissipate the casting energy sufficiently, and either the fly will land on the water too harshly or the leader will kick or tuck at the end of a cast.

Tippet size is described according to either its breaking strength (pound-test) or material thickness (X value). For tapered leaders, I generally rely on the X value, because each of the alphanumeric designations remains constant for a corresponding diameter regardless of the line manufacturer; for example, all 3X tippets have a .008-inch diameter. In contrast, the correlation between breaking strength and diameter is inexact and varies from one manufacturer to another. For example, Brand A's 10-pound-test tippet may be .009 inch in diameter, whereas Brand B's is .012 inch. The difference between the diameters of Brands A and B can determine whether a tapered leader-fly combination unrolls properly. That's why the X value system is a more accurate indicator of diameter than is breaking strength.

For quality presentations, some fly fishers rely on the "rule of 4" to match a fly to an appropriate tippet X value. They advocate dividing the hook size by 4 to arrive at the correct tippet size. For instance, a fly tied on a size 12 hook would call for a 3X tippet (12 ÷ 4 = 3).

Although this system can be very helpful, it is by no means a "rule," because a fly that is bulkier or lighter than the norm may require a thicker or thinner tippet. For example, if the rule of 4 indicates a 2X tippet for an average-size fly tied on a size 8 hook ($8 \div 4 = 2$), a thicker 1X tippet could be a better choice if the pattern is heavily dressed or weighted, and a thinner 3X tippet might perform better on a lighter or more streamlined fly. Another shortcoming of this method is that when hooks larger than size 2 are divided by 4, the quotient is less than 1; therefore, all that can be determined is that the tippet should be 0X or greater.

Some fly fishers rely instead on an equally arbitrary "rule of 3," whereby the hook size is divided by 3 instead of 4 to determine the tippet size. Considering their limitations, the rules of 4 and 3 should serve only as guidelines in selecting tippet size, but each can offer an excellent starting point if you factor in a fly's weight and wind resistance as well.

The leader section that attaches to the fly line is called the butt. For maximum performance, the diameter of the butt section should be approximately 75 percent of the thickness of the fly-line tip. It should also be similar in flexibility.

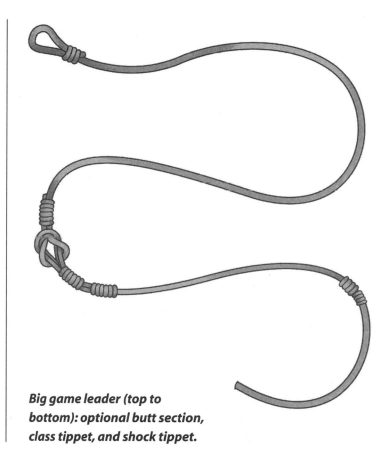

Big game leader (top to bottom): optional butt section, class tippet, and shock tippet.

BIG-GAME LEADERS

Big-game, or tarpon, leaders are generally used for heavy-duty saltwater fly fishing. They have a tippet section often referred to as a class tippet, which is knotted to a thicker shock tippet that helps prevent break-offs from tough-mouthed fish such as tarpon and sailfish. For example, a 16-pound-test class tippet might be knotted to an 80-pound-test shock tippet. (A shock tippet of 12 inches or less can also be attached to a tapered leader when necessary.) Whereas tippet differences among tapered leaders are usually measured in thousandths of an inch and identified according to their X value, minuscule fractions of an inch are not a factor in selecting the class tippets for big-game leaders. These are always referred to in terms of breaking strength or pound-test, up to a maximum allowable 20-pound-test according to International Game Fish Association fly-fishing regulations. A fly is matched to the class tippet breaking strength that will best achieve the desired presentation: 20-pound-test for the largest flies, 12- to 16-pound-test for less bulky patterns, and so forth.

In some circumstances, the presentation is a secondary consideration. For instance, establishing a fly-fishing class tippet record for an especially large fish species (e.g., tarpon or muskie) may require that an extremely light tippet, as delicate as 2-pound-test, be matched to a disproportionately large fly and shock tippet that is virtually impossible to cast efficiently or turn over properly.

Big-game leaders are sometimes connected to a heavier butt section just like their tapered counterparts. In situations where a relatively silent presentation is necessary to avoid scaring fish near the surface, a butt section is commonly used in conjunction with a floating fly line. One is seldom needed with a sinking line, however, because the targeted fish are usually deep enough that they are unaffected by the presentation.

LEVEL LEADERS

As the name indicates, a level leader is a single strand of monofilament that has no taper. Some fly fishers use a short level section (sometimes well under 5 feet long) with a sinking fly line to reduce any "belly" in the line and provide more direct contact with the fly. However, a level leader does not cast or present the fly as proficiently as a well-designed tapered leader, and those problems become magnified as casting distance increases. As a result, a level leader is an especially poor choice when combined with a floating line.

PRACTICE LEADERS

Old and damaged leaders can be recycled for practice sessions. I recommend using a tapered leader between 7 and 10 feet long, because it will cast smoother than either a level or big-game leader. To simulate the action of casting a fly, some fly fishers like to attach either a fly with the hook bend cut off or a tiny piece of yarn to the leader for practicing on a lawn. Because both tend to get hung up in the grass, I rarely use either one of them unless I'm casting to targets. If you opt for yarn or a fly for practice, make sure they are matched as closely as possible to the leader tippet for a good turnover.

You can also build a high-performance, four-piece tapered leader by using the 50 Percent Step-Down Leader Formula, which includes these five basic elements:

1. The butt section is 50 percent, or half, of the overall length of the leader. (The *intended* length will vary slightly from the *exact* length of the finished leader.)
2. The second, "decrease," section is 50 percent, or half, of the length of the butt.
3. The third, "taper," section is 50 percent, or half, of the length of the second.
4. The tippet section should be about 18 to 24 inches long to allow for tying on a fly or piece of yarn.
5. All monofilament should be premium spinning line of the same manufacturer to ensure consistency in diameter and flexibility for top performance.

As an example, the following are instructions to construct a leader that's approximately 10 feet long for 8-, 9-, and 10-weight lines using the above formula. (It is not critical that each measurement be exact.) Secure all lengths together with blood knots. Starting with a 5-foot butt section that is either 50-pound-test or .028 inch in diameter, add a 2 $\frac{1}{2}$-foot-long piece that is either 40-pound-test or .024 inch in diameter. Follow with a third section 1.25 feet long that is either 25-pound-test or .020 inch in diameter, and then attach a 01X or 10-pound-test tippet that is 24 inches long.

two

Casting Position

The Grip

The manner in which a rod is held can significantly affect casting performance. Therefore, the proper grip is the foundation of a good casting stroke, whereas an inferior grip can lead to problems. With varying degrees of effectiveness, fly fishers almost always hold a rod by using some variation of an index-finger-on-top, V, or thumb-on-top grip.

Holding a rod with the index finger on top of the cork handle may prove satisfactory for making short casts of less than 50 feet or so with light trout and panfish rods, but it does not provide the kind of leverage needed to consistently throw a long line, make an especially sharp backcast, or cast with heavy rods such as those used for large saltwater fish. Similarly, a V grip lacks sufficient leverage on the forward cast compared with the thumb-on-top position. Consequently, casters using a V grip will often finish the backcast with the hand in a palm-up position, and then turn the palm over to complete the forward cast. Since this palm-up, palm-down rotation doesn't support the wrist properly the way a thumb-on-top grip does, the wrist has a tendency to either break or roll during a cast, and a wide semicircular loop results. This wrist motion occurs most often on the forward stroke, but it can happen on the backcast as well.

In comparison with other grips, a dominant thumb placement provides better leverage, increased accuracy, more comfort, higher line speed, firmer stops, and the versatility to be used with a wide variety of casts. But there is much more to the thumb-on-top grip than simply placing the thumb in a dominant position on the handle.

To correctly establish the grip, the rod must be held primarily in the fingers and not the palm of the hand. Begin by placing the cork grip at the base of both the little and ring fingers so that it extends diagonally across the second knuckle of the middle finger to the first knuckle of the index finger. Then lay the thumb flat across the top of the cork until it is 180 degrees opposite the guides and the first knuckle of the index finger. Furthermore, the index finger should extend forward so that it is almost even with the tip of the thumb and hooked slightly, trigger-finger style, around the cork handle. As the observant and accomplished young fly fisher Susannah Mann points out, the correct grip is similar to the one used to hold a flashlight.

In this extended hook position, the index finger provides excellent leverage necessary for good acceleration and a sharp backcast. With the rod held primarily in the bottom three fingers of the casting hand, you use the hooked index finger to simultaneously lift line and pull the rod back on the pickup and to provide continued leverage on each

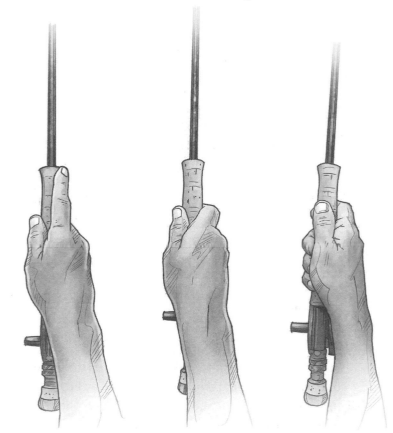

Grips (left to right): index-finger-on-top, V, thumb-on-top.

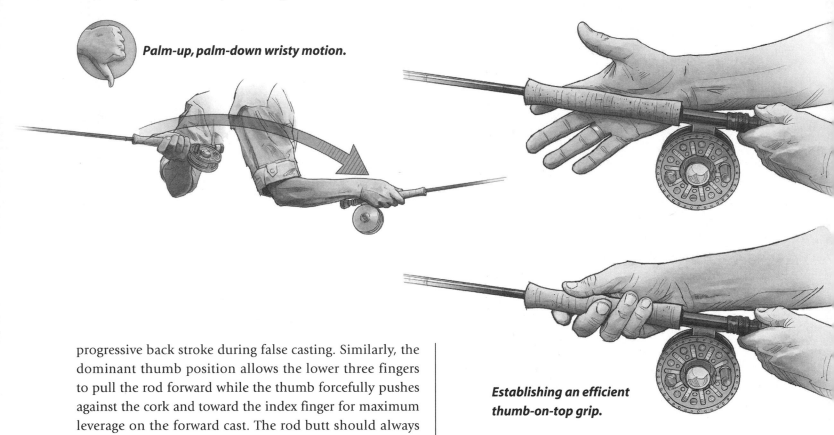

Palm-up, palm-down wristy motion.

Establishing an efficient thumb-on-top grip.

progressive back stroke during false casting. Similarly, the dominant thumb position allows the lower three fingers to pull the rod forward while the thumb forcefully pushes against the cork and toward the index finger for maximum leverage on the forward cast. The rod butt should always be situated on the inside part of the forearm, because an

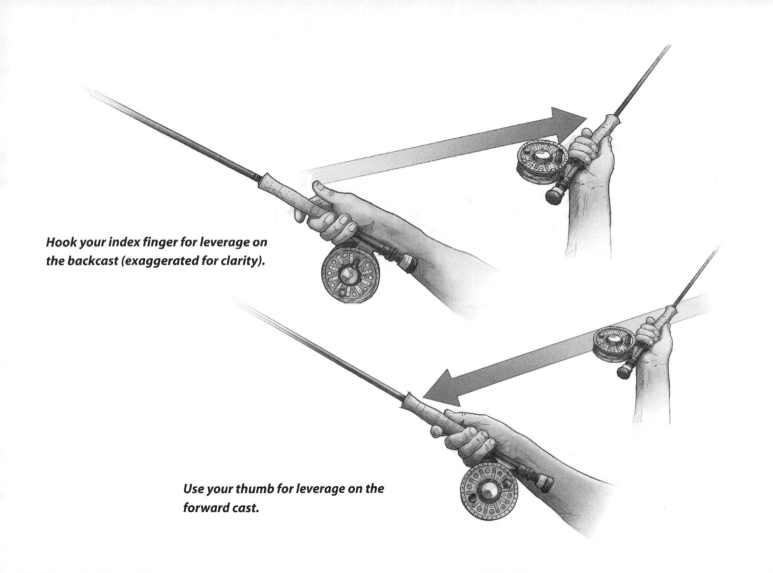

Hook your index finger for leverage on the backcast (exaggerated for clarity).

Use your thumb for leverage on the forward cast.

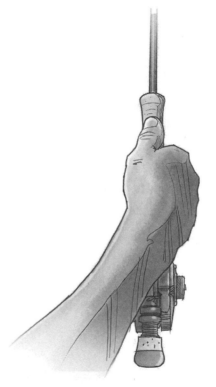

The rod butt should be situated to the inside part of the forearm.

A wristy motion can develop if the butt is held underneath (middle) or protruding to the outside (right) of the forearm.

inefficient wristy motion is most likely develop if the butt is held underneath or protruding to the outside of the forearm.

Some fly fishers mistakenly believe that the thumb must face completely toward the target throughout the backcast. Although that's possible on short casts where the rod is held vertically in a "straight-up" style of casting, some supination, or upward rotation of the palm and forearm, naturally occurs as the stroke lengthens. Nevertheless, a portion of the thumb, no matter how small, should always remain behind the cork to provide even the slightest degree of leverage when the forward stroke begins. That being said, however, it is undesirable to twist or rotate the wrist outward on the backcast, because the thumb will not be in a position to provide sufficient leverage on the forward cast. At the other extreme, rigidly bending the wrist inward to keep the entire thumb behind the cork grip will create excessive muscle tension in the hand and forearm, which will lead to fatigue.

Over the years, I've noticed that casters who hold the cork grip roughly parallel with the base of the fingers or across the heartline of the palm often develop a wristy casting motion. Likewise, placing the entire heel of the hand on

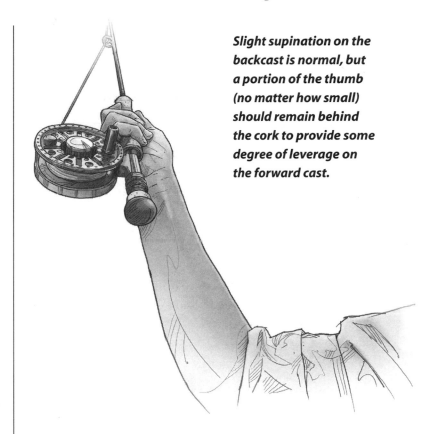

Slight supination on the backcast is normal, but a portion of the thumb (no matter how small) should remain behind the cork to provide some degree of leverage on the forward cast.

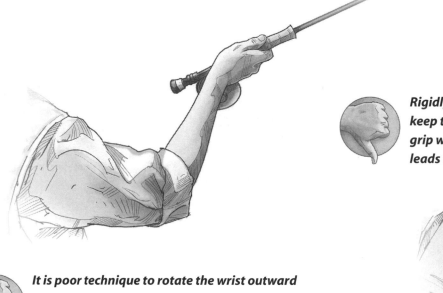

Rigidly bending the wrist inward to keep the entire thumb behind the cork grip will create muscle tension that leads to fatigue.

It is poor technique to rotate the wrist outward on the backcast because the thumb will not be in a position to provide sufficient leverage for the forward cast.

top of the cork also results in excessive use of the wrist. In their frustration to eliminate wrist-associated problems, some fly fishers resort to commercial gadgets, tape, and even holding the rod butt against the inside of the forearm to lock the wrist in place, when all that may be needed is a simple adjustment to the way they grip the rod.

Even the tension with which the rod is grasped has a bearing on casting performance. The grip should be firm yet

The Line Hand

The line hand should be positioned slightly below and in alignment with the rod hand. The hands should never appreciably separate *throughout* a cast unless a haul is executed, after which the line hand always returns to its original location just beneath and directly in line with the rod hand. (See Chapter 6 for more details.)

Placing the entire heel of the hand on top of the cork grip can result in a wristy casting motion.

relaxed, but certainly not a white-knuckle or "death" grip. The tension should approximate that of securely holding on to a small bird without crushing it. If the knuckles are white, the grip is too tight.

The line hand should be positioned slightly below and in alignment with the rod hand.

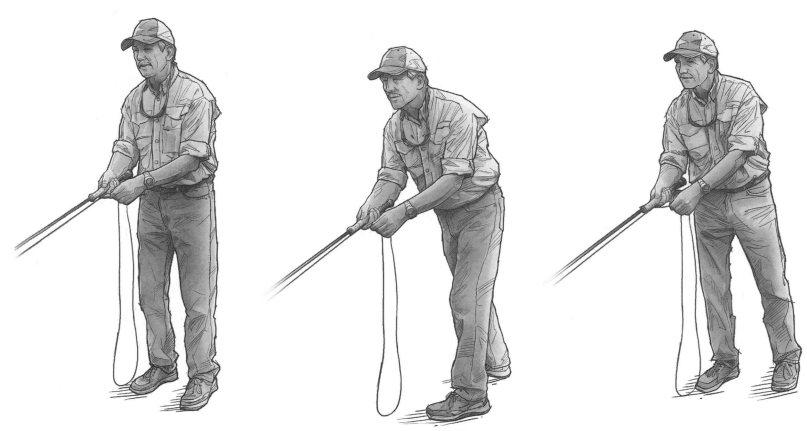

Stances (left to right): square stance, open stance, and closed stance.

The Stance

Three popular stances are used in fly casting: square, open, and closed. In a square stance, feet and shoulders are aligned perpendicular to the direction of the cast. The closed stance is similar to the square position except that the foot closer to the cast is situated slightly in front of the other foot. With an open stance, the feet are almost parallel to the casting direction, with the back foot slightly closer to that alignment than the front one. Regardless of which stance you choose, your feet should be spread at a comfortable distance—roughly shoulder width apart.

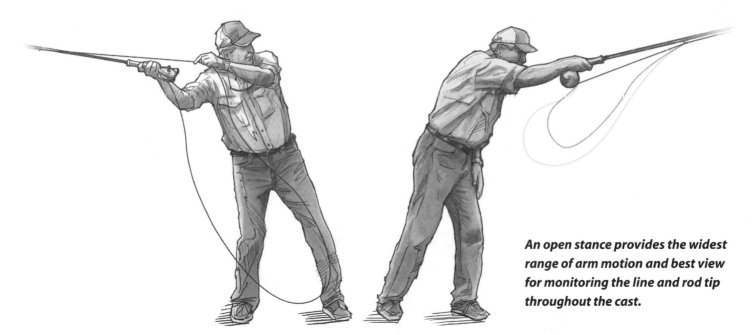

An open stance provides the widest range of arm motion and best view for monitoring the line and rod tip throughout the cast.

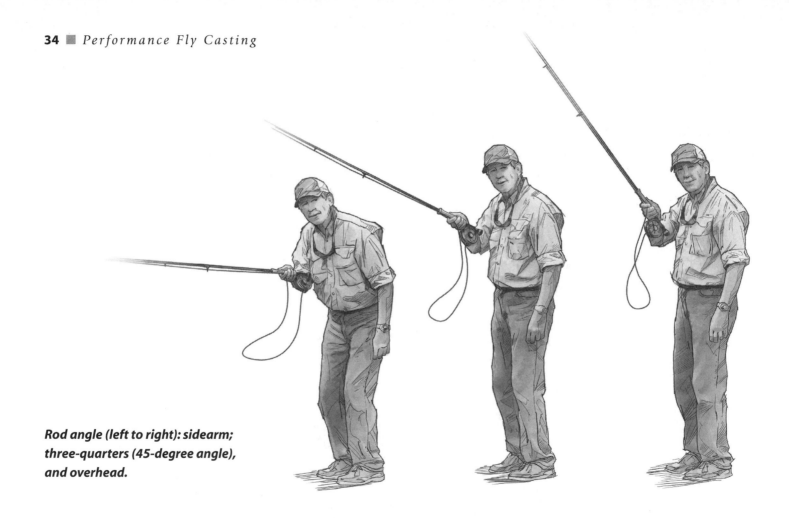

Rod angle (left to right): sidearm; three-quarters (45-degree angle), and overhead.

Although I use all three stances to one degree or another, I recommend a slightly open position in most instances, because it provides the widest range of arm motion with the potential for the longest casting stroke. Likewise, an open stance gives the best overall view of the line and rod tip throughout the cast so that you can readily monitor them when necessary. However, the other two stances allow better shoulder rotation for additional torque during the casting stroke.

Rod Angle and Elbow Position

The simplest way to develop a good casting stroke is to start with the elbow positioned close to the body and the rod canted slightly off to the side at about a 45-degree angle. With the rod at this "three-quarters" slant, the fly line, rod tip, and arm movement are much easier to observe than when the rod is held vertically. Consequently, you can more readily identify and rectify any problems. Furthermore, a three-quarter position gives your arm the broadest range of motion, which in turn allows for a longer and more fluid stroke. In the process, you'll find that long casts are easier to achieve and require less effort with the lengthier stroke.

Once you've developed a proficient casting motion with the rod at a 45-degree angle, it is relatively simple to change to either a more sidearm or overhead cast simply by keeping the elbow in the same relaxed position close to the body, and then raising or lowering the forearm to a more vertical or horizontal position as needed.

three

The Vertical Plane

TO PRACTICE SOME OF the earliest fly-casting styles, the angler was encouraged to hold a book, or even a stone in at least one instance, between the casting arm and body so that the elbow would remain stationary. Using the numbers on a clock as reference points, the caster was then directed to make a forward cast and backcast by stopping the rod, like the hands of a clock, at specific hour positions—usually between nine and one o'clock or ten and two o'clock. That's a poor analogy for the motion a rod should make during the casting stroke. A clock face is round because the hands rotate around a center axis point. If a rod likewise pivots about a single stationary axis point, such as the elbow or wrist, the tip will move in an acute arc that produces ineffi-cient sagging loops loaded with slack. That's because the fly line always follows the direction in which the rod tip is moving during the casting stroke. Furthermore, proponents of "clock casting" do not take into account that those angles, or hour positions, change significantly based on the length of line being cast as well as the loop's direction and degree of incline.

Proficient fly casting is the process of using a weighted line to load a rod and thereby form aerodynamically shaped loops that unroll on back and forward strokes. To achieve that end, you must be familiar with the universal elements that pertain to all sound casting strokes: the acceleration and speedup phase; the stop; the straight line; the loop;

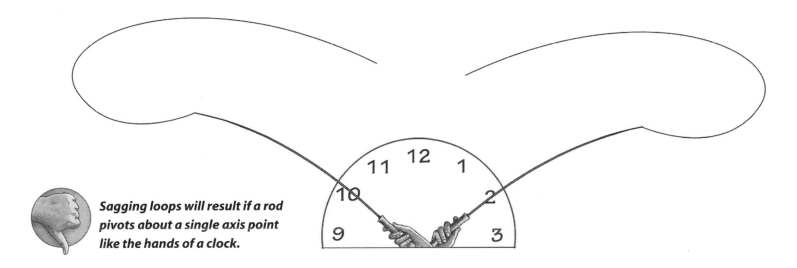

Sagging loops will result if a rod pivots about a single axis point like the hands of a clock.

length of the casting stroke; loading the rod; shooting line; the drop; elimination of slack; tracking (see Chapter 4); and the pickup (see Chapter 5). Understanding and mastering these fundamental components of a cast is like following a recipe, and any attempt to shortcut the prescribed formula will yield poor results. It's also important that these elements be applied with the same degree of emphasis on both backcast and forward cast.

Acceleration and Speedup Phase

For the purposes of executing an efficient cast, acceleration is defined as steadily and smoothly increasing the speed of the rod throughout the casting stroke in order to build corresponding velocity in the line. Immediately preceding the

Proficient fly casting is the process of using a weighted line to load a rod and thereby form aerodynamically shaped loops that unroll on the forward casts and backcasts.

stop, or end of the casting motion, acceleration of the rod tip should increase sharply at an exponential rate so that maximum speed is achieved precisely as the stroke is completed.

This brief exponential speedup of the tip can be referred to as the turnover, power stroke, flipping the tip, speed stroke, whumping the rod, power snap, or speedup and stop. These terms can be confusing or easily misunderstood, because they unintentionally imply an action somewhat

disconnected from the rest of the acceleration phase. However, although the speedup part of the stroke is often referred to separately, it must nevertheless be a *smooth* and *seamless* part of the entire acceleration phase. It is important to note that the direction the rod tip is moving during the speedup determines the direction in which the loop unrolls.

The purpose of the acceleration and speedup phase is to load, or bend, the rod under the weight of the moving fly line. Furthermore, the bend is directly proportional to the

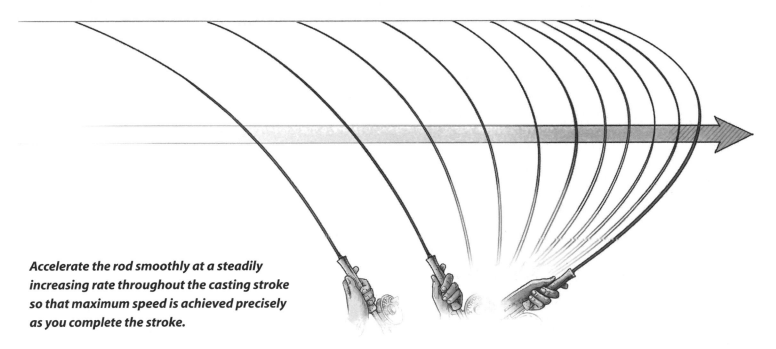

Accelerate the rod smoothly at a steadily increasing rate throughout the casting stroke so that maximum speed is achieved precisely as you complete the stroke.

increasing velocity of the casting stroke and the corresponding speed of the weighted line. If the acceleration and speedup phase is performed correctly, the rod will progressively bend throughout the stroke so that maximum load-

ing is achieved just before the stop at the end of each forward cast and backcast.

Moving the rod as quickly as possible from the beginning of the cast to the end is an ineffective way to load the

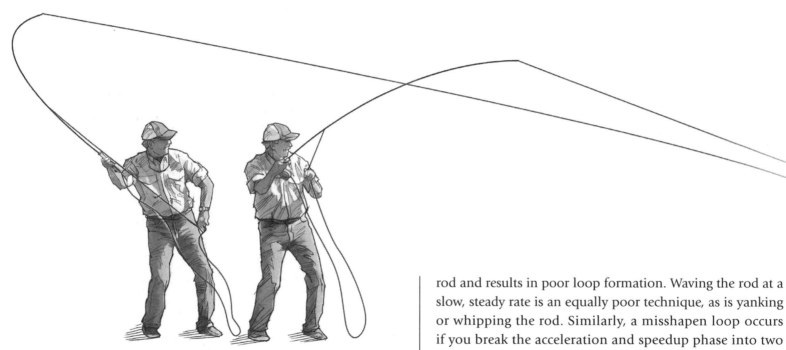

rod and results in poor loop formation. Waving the rod at a slow, steady rate is an equally poor technique, as is yanking or whipping the rod. Similarly, a misshapen loop occurs if you break the acceleration and speedup phase into two separate motions by moving the rod rather slowly at the beginning of the cast and then giving it a sudden, distinctly separate burst of speed at the end.

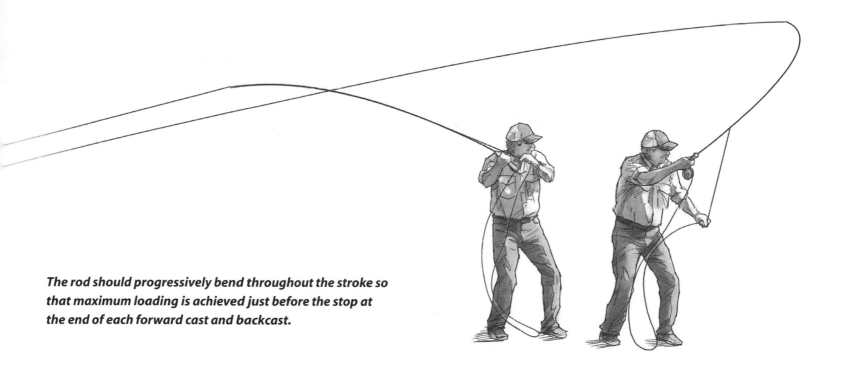

The rod should progressively bend throughout the stroke so that maximum loading is achieved just before the stop at the end of each forward cast and backcast.

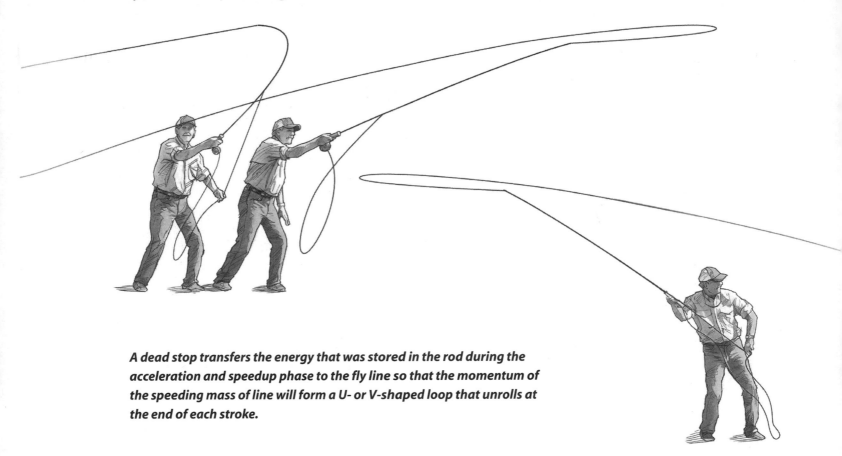

A dead stop transfers the energy that was stored in the rod during the acceleration and speedup phase to the fly line so that the momentum of the speeding mass of line will form a U- or V-shaped loop that unrolls at the end of each stroke.

The Stop

The single most important factor leading to the creation of a loop is a firm, yet smooth stop of the rod at the completion of each forward and back stroke. A dead stop transfers the energy that was stored in the rod during the acceleration and speedup phase to the fly line, so that the momentum of the speeding mass of weighted line will form a U- or V-shaped loop that unrolls at the end of each stroke. Failure to execute a complete stop will result in an inferior loop, and in many instances, no loop is formed regardless of how much the rod is accelerated. Under these circumstances, the line may fail to completely unroll.

The stop is analogous to stopping a car smoothly. Continuous intense pressure on a car's brake pedal will cause a vehicle to first lurch forward and then snap backward as

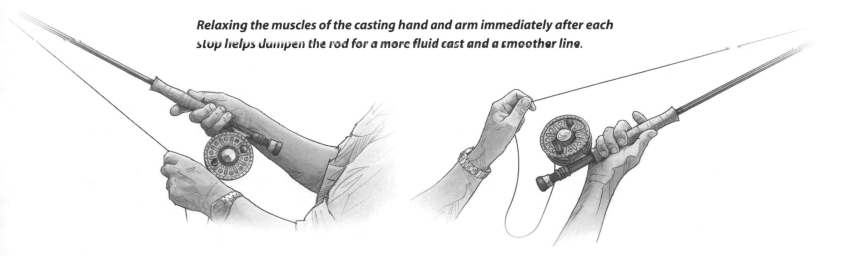

Relaxing the muscles of the casting hand and arm immediately after each stop helps dampen the rod for a more fluid cast and a smoother line.

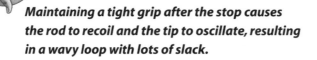

Maintaining a tight grip after the stop causes the rod to recoil and the tip to oscillate, resulting in a wavy loop with lots of slack.

it comes to an abrupt halt. However, simply easing or relaxing foot pressure on the pedal just as the car comes to a standstill will soften the stop. Similarly, relaxing the muscles of the casting hand and arm immediately after each stop helps dampen the rod for a more fluid cast and smoother line. Conversely, maintaining a tight grip with the casting hand after the stop causes the rod to recoil and the tip to oscillate, resulting in a wavy loop with lots of slack.

The Straight Line

The basic geometric principle "the shortest distance between two points is a straight line" is a key element to good casting. With that axiom in mind, you should accelerate the rod tip in a straight-line path between the stopping points at the end of the backcast and the forward cast. Once you stop the rod to complete the casting stroke, the fly line's momentum will cause it to unroll ahead of the tip and form a loop.

Because the loop always unrolls in the direction in which the rod tip is moving during the speedup, maintaining a linear path during this portion of the casting stroke is absolutely critical to good loop formation. A sagging loop with its ensuing slack will result if the path is arced or if the rod tip otherwise drops below a straight-line path before the stop.

Optimally, the trajectory of the fly line on the forward cast should be 180 degrees opposite the trajectory of the

Accelerate the rod tip in a straight-line path between the stopping points at the end of the backcast and the forward cast.

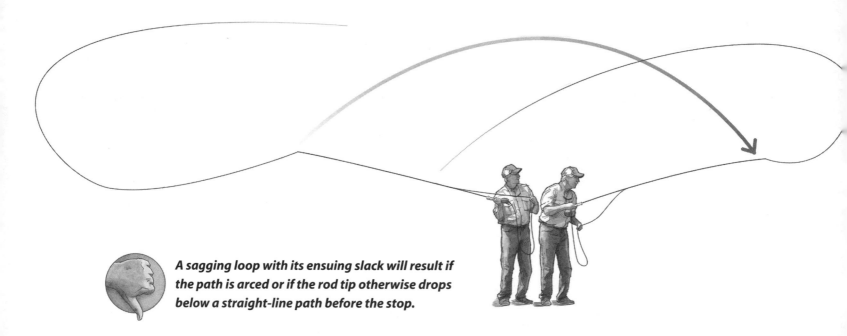

A sagging loop with its ensuing slack will result if the path is arced or if the rod tip otherwise drops below a straight-line path before the stop.

backcast. The angle of trajectory can be adjusted slightly depending on whether a high or low forward cast is desired. For example, when a high forward cast is necessary either to throw a long line or take advantage of a tailwind, the back-cast should slant down 180 degrees in the opposite direction, and when a low forward cast is needed, the backcast should slant upward.

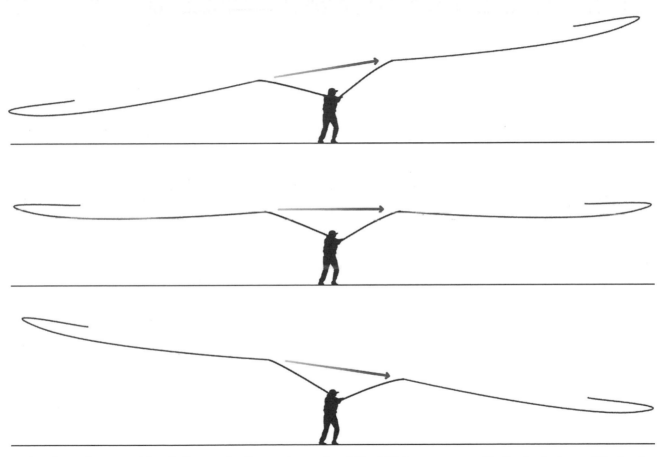

Optimally, the trajectory of the fly line on the forward cast should be 180 degrees opposite the trajectory of the backcast.

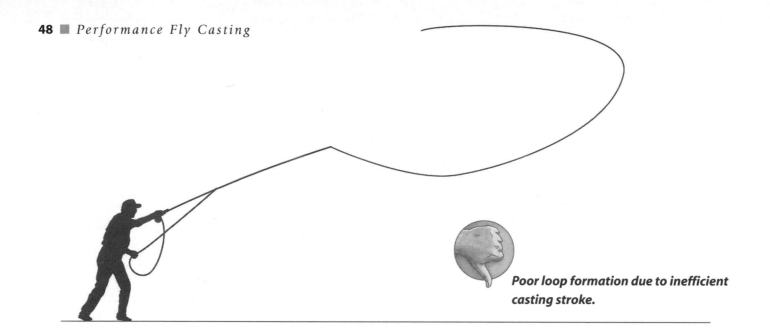

Poor loop formation due to inefficient casting stroke.

The Loop

Good loop formation is the cornerstone of performance casting. Therefore, creating a loop, managing its shape, and controlling its velocity should be the ultimate objectives in any fly-fishing situation, whether you're making an extra-long cast or a short one. The ideal loop has a U or V shape and at least enough velocity for the line to unroll smoothly with no discernible shock waves in it. Although a tight loop is generally considered to be the product of a highly efficient cast, on some occasions a more open loop is preferable, such as when casting weighted flies or trying to make a gentle presentation.

Loop shape and size are largely determined by the char-

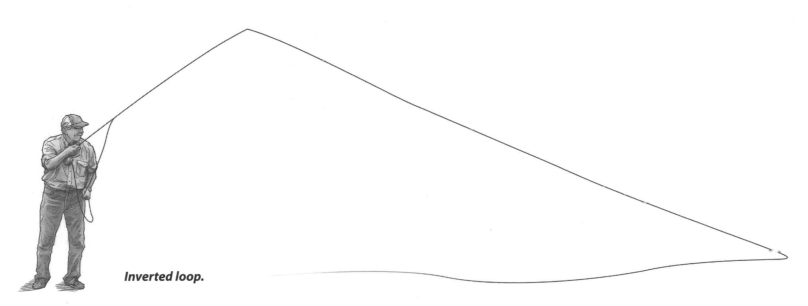

Inverted loop.

acteristics of the speedup, the stop, and the horizontal path of the rod tip. The quicker and shorter the speedup, the firmer the stop, and the straighter the path of the casting stroke, the tighter the loop will be, and vice versa (Compare the loop sizes in the illustrations on pages 42 and 48.) A loop may not form as the result of one or more of the following: a soft stop or no stop at all; an insufficient accel-

eration and speedup phase; a semicircular or severely arced casting stroke; or the rod being moved as quickly as possible from start to finish.

At the discretion of the caster, a loop can be situated anywhere between a vertical over-the-top position and one that is slanted off to the side. Some circumstances may even require an inverted loop.

Length of the Casting Stroke

There is a direct correlation between the amount of line being cast and the appropriate length of the casting stroke. As the length of line increases, a corresponding lengthening

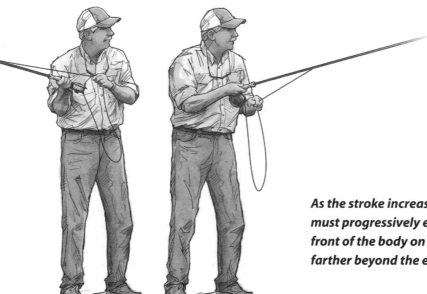

As the stroke increases in length, the casting hand must progressively extend a greater distance in front of the body on the forward cast and reach farther beyond the elbow on the backcast.

of the stroke is also needed. In other words, a long line requires a long stroke, and a short line calls for a proportionately shorter stroke. Furthermore, as the stroke increases in length, the casting hand must progressively extend a greater distance in front of the body on the forward cast and reach farther beyond the elbow on the backcast.

When using a long casting stroke, you have the potential to make a longer cast and build more line speed with significantly less effort than a short motion allows. Additionally, the inherent fluidity of a long stroke makes it much easier to form smooth, slack-free loops than if you use a constricted stroke, with its abrupt and jerky nature.

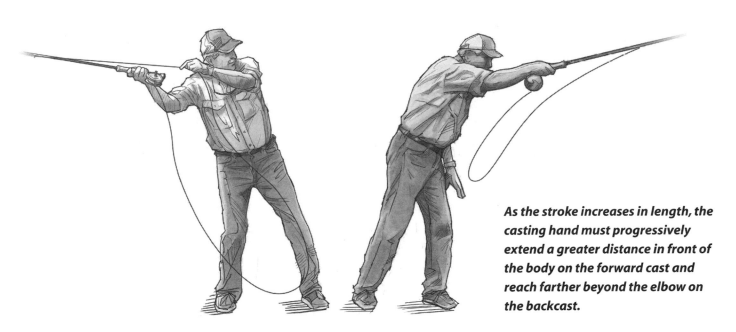

As the stroke increases in length, the casting hand must progressively extend a greater distance in front of the body on the forward cast and reach farther beyond the elbow on the backcast.

Loading the Rod

In theory, a rod is supposed to optimally load under the weight of the forward 30-foot section of the designated fly line. With modern rods and line tapers, however, that length can vary considerably with each of the different tapers and from one rod to another. It also differs from caster to caster, as well as with each set of circumstances. Finding the ideal length of line, or "sweet spot," for a particular rod requires practice time to gain familiarity with the rod and line combination.

In order for the rod to load, or bend, under the weight of the line, ample time must be allowed for the loop to sufficiently unroll after the completion of either the forward or back stroke, as the case may be. That time varies with the amount of line being cast and the speed at which it is trav-

eling. The longer the line or the slower it is moving, the greater the pause, whereas the shorter the line or the faster it is moving, the briefer the pause.

The rod will not load if you try to aerialize more fly line than you are capable of straightening. That doesn't mean that the line should completely unroll on the backcast and forward cast, only that it is capable of straightening under its own momentum. As a matter of fact, the rod actually bends under its maximum load just before the loop straightens and while there is still some minimal curvature at the extreme end of the line. At that point, the end of the fly line has a slight hook or J shape as the rod tip flexes under the line's weight. That's the precise moment to begin the next progressive stroke.

Too many individuals guess as to when their rod is loaded and usually end up waiting too long or not long

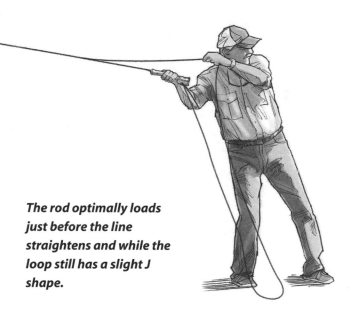

enough. Either way, the rod does not load adequately for a high-performance cast. You can take out the guesswork and eventually acquire an instinctive feel for when the rod is loaded by religiously watching the rod tip or fly line throughout the entire cast, especially during practice sessions. Only after developing a keen sense of timing can you focus on the fishing at hand and still have total confidence that the rod is loading optimally.

A snap or pop that sounds like a cracking whip is an indication that the cast was started before the loop straightened sufficiently for the rod to load. By comparison, if the line completely straightens, the rod tip will lose its bend and recoil to an erect position. A corresponding bumping sensation can be detected in the rod as it reacts to the loop completely unrolling.

The rod optimally loads just before the line straightens and while the loop still has a slight J shape.

A snap or pop that sounds like a whip cracking indicates that the cast was started before the loop straightened sufficiently for the rod to load.

"Snap"

If the line completely straightens, the rod tip will lose its bend.

Shooting Line

In order to deliver the fly toward a designated target, you should shoot line on each progressive false cast until the rod is loaded with sufficient length and weight to make the final presentation. To make a presentation in excess of 30 feet, work the fly line out by false casting until the rod is loaded at the line's sweet spot, then shoot the remaining length of line toward the target.

In all situations, false casting should be reduced to the minimum number of strokes needed to achieve a desired distance. The more strokes required, the greater the chance for mistakes and the more time required to make a presentation. Although many casters shoot only on the forward stroke, releasing line also on the backcast is just as desirable, because it substantially reduces the number of false casts needed to reach the target. As a matter of fact, shooting a substantial length of line on the final backcast can play an integral role in long-distance casting.

Precise timing is necessary to shoot line optimally. The line must be released from the line hand precisely at the completion of the casting stroke. Letting go too early produces slack that will destroy the cast, whereas the line won't go anywhere if the release is delayed. When the rod is properly loaded, you can feel the slight pull of the line the instant it's ready to shoot.

In some situations, it's advantageous to false-cast without shooting any line. One of the most notable occurs when trying to hover a fly over a target in order to gauge the accuracy of a presentation. Another such situation arises when a floating fly absorbs so much water that it sinks and performing a series of short, quick false casts will help dry the fly. Small pieces of debris that collect on the fly, leader, and line can be removed the same way.

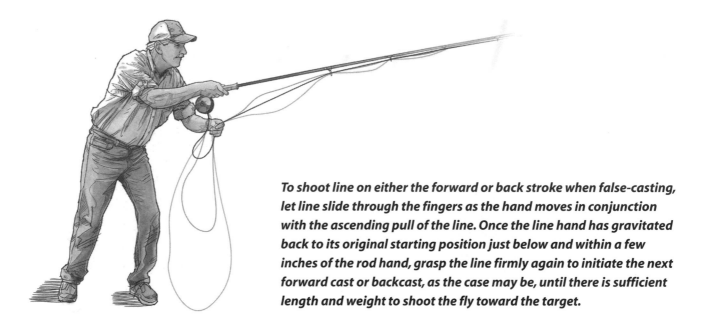

To shoot line on either the forward or back stroke when false-casting, let line slide through the fingers as the hand moves in conjunction with the ascending pull of the line. Once the line hand has gravitated back to its original starting position just below and within a few inches of the rod hand, grasp the line firmly again to initiate the next forward cast or backcast, as the case may be, until there is sufficient length and weight to shoot the fly toward the target.

The Drop

After the stop at the completion of the final forward presentation cast, the rod tip should be lowered, or dropped, slowly to the surface as the loop unrolls over the water. Otherwise, an undesirable belly of slack line forms between the elevated rod tip and the line's contact point with the water. The drop eliminates that sag and allows you to maintain a direct straight-line connection with the end of the line so that you are immediately ready to either start another cast or set the hook on a fish the moment the fly touches the water.

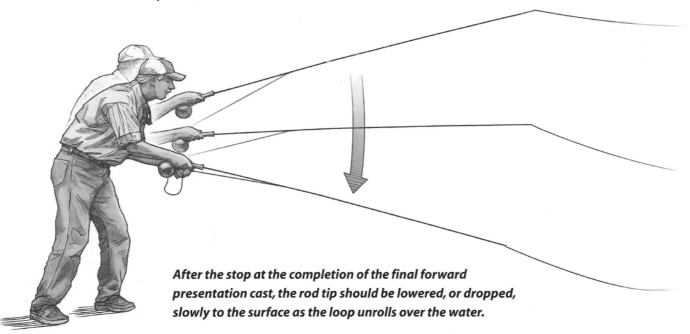

After the stop at the completion of the final forward presentation cast, the rod tip should be lowered, or dropped, slowly to the surface as the loop unrolls over the water.

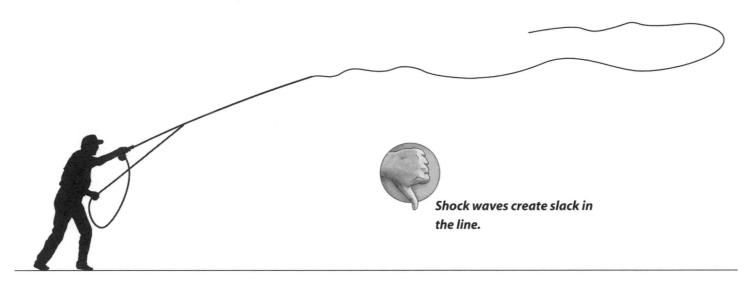

Shock waves create slack in the line.

Elimination of Slack

If I could break fly casting down to the simplest explanation, it would be "keep the rod bent (or loaded) under the weight of the fly line." But that's possible only if the line is slack-free. The elimination of slack is a recurrent theme throughout this text and should be a primary objective for every serious fly caster. Slack, or lack of line tension, decreases a caster's ability to maintain contact with and control of the entire fly line. As a result, *slack reduces the effective length of the casting stroke.*

With slack in the line, a portion of the acceleration and speedup phase is ineffective because it involves taking up that slack during the casting stroke. The more slack there is,

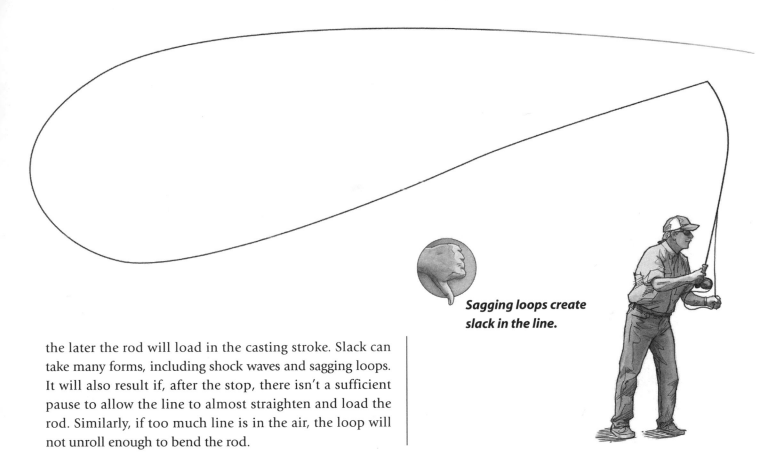

Sagging loops create slack in the line.

the later the rod will load in the casting stroke. Slack can take many forms, including shock waves and sagging loops. It will also result if, after the stop, there isn't a sufficient pause to allow the line to almost straighten and load the rod. Similarly, if too much line is in the air, the loop will not unroll enough to bend the rod.

Slack forms if there isn't a sufficient pause after the stop to allow the line to almost straighten and load the rod.

four

The Tracking Plane

IN TRYING TO FINE-TUNE their individual casting strokes, many fly casters tend to focus on the vertical plane and the rod's position as it moves between the forward cast and backcast. But one perspective of the cast that is frequently ignored is what I refer to as the tracking plane, a position that looks directly down the length of the rod shaft from the tip, whether the rod is held vertically for an overhead cast, horizontally for a sidearm cast, or tilted somewhere in between. The tracking plane is sometimes called the horizontal plane, a misnomer unless the rod path is directly overhead.

Ideally, the tip should track in a straight line, the shortest distance from point A to point B when executing a basic cast. That doesn't mean that both the forward cast and the backcast have to follow the same linear path, only that a straight line should be maintained during each acceleration and speedup phase until the stop is completed. Then, at your discretion, the track can be changed by shifting the rod angle either slightly or significantly while the line unfurls after the stop. For example, a Belgian or elliptical cast is executed by tilting the rod to the side for the back stroke and then moving it slowly, after the stop, to a more vertical position for the forward presentation.

Poor tracking is caused by moving the rod along a curved path during the acceleration and speedup phase. That's because the rod forms a radius as it swings about an

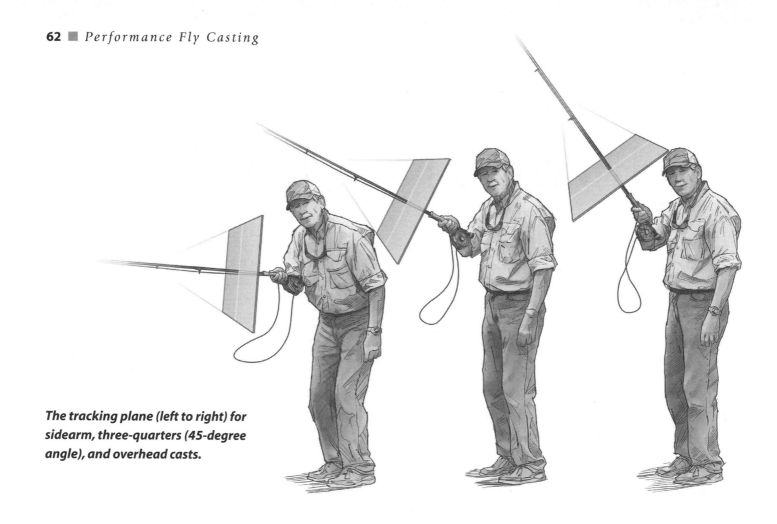

The tracking plane (left to right) for sidearm, three-quarters (45-degree angle), and overhead casts.

The rod tip should track in a straight line, in this case, looking down the shaft of the rod held at a three-quarters (45-degree) angle.

axis point like a gate pivoting on a hinge. Usually that hinge point will be the shoulder, elbow, or wrist joint, but it can also be any combination of those components.

Some anglers have a propensity to come out of the track on both the backcast and forward cast. Others hook the rod around the body primarily during only one portion of the casting stroke. But the results are the same. Even the slightest variation from a straight-line track during the acceleration and speedup phase will cause unwanted slack that prevents the rod from loading adequately. Eliminating that slack will not only load the rod properly, but result in more accurate casts as well.

Many casters experience tracking problems because they hold the rod a considerable distance from the body throughout the cast, as sometimes happens when they try to avoid being hit by either the line or the fly—especially if the wind is blowing toward the casting shoulder. However, the farther the arm is extended, the greater the probability that it will form a radius that causes the rod to swing in an arc. Furthermore, holding the rod too far from the body also shortens the effective straight-line length of the casting stroke, which in turn makes it more difficult to fully load the rod and make good stops. Consequently, keeping the hand and elbow relatively close to the body makes

for better tracking, allows you to make longer straight-line strokes, and provides the additional leverage required for the most efficient acceleration and speedup and the firmest stop.

In the worst example of a curved track, the arm remains relatively rigid and stationary while the body twists around from front to back to accelerate the rod. The body's motion produces a sweeping, swinging action of the rod that pre-

The Belgian or elliptical cast tracks from a sidearm backcast to an overhead path on the forward cast.

vents it from ever making a good stop—arguably the most important part of the cast.

It is critical that you be able to assess the tracking path in order to spot any problems. Minor deviations from a linear track are much more difficult to identify, so it pays to monitor various aspects of your cast carefully. Watching the joints of the shoulder, elbow, and wrist for any signs of hinging is a good place to start. Checking the path of the rod tip can also reveal problems. In addition, poor tracking will result in the fly line not landing perfectly straight at the completion of the forward stroke. However, probably the best tracking indicator is the thumb tip, provided you are using a proper thumb-on-top grip. Because the tips of both the rod and thumb will parallel one another during a cast, any straight-line deviation of the rod can be quickly detected by watching the thumb tip's tracking path.

The arm will form a radius and the rod will not track in a straight line if the shoulder is used as an axis point.

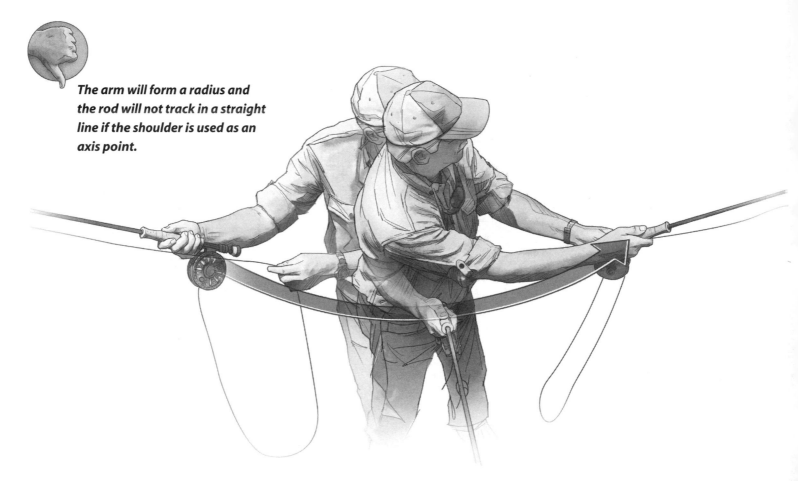

 If the elbow remains stationary, it will serve as an axis point and the forearm will form a radius so that the rod will only move in a curved path during the casting stroke.

 Swinging the rod hand back and forth at the wrist, like a gate pivoting on a hinge, prohibits the rod from travelling in a straight line.

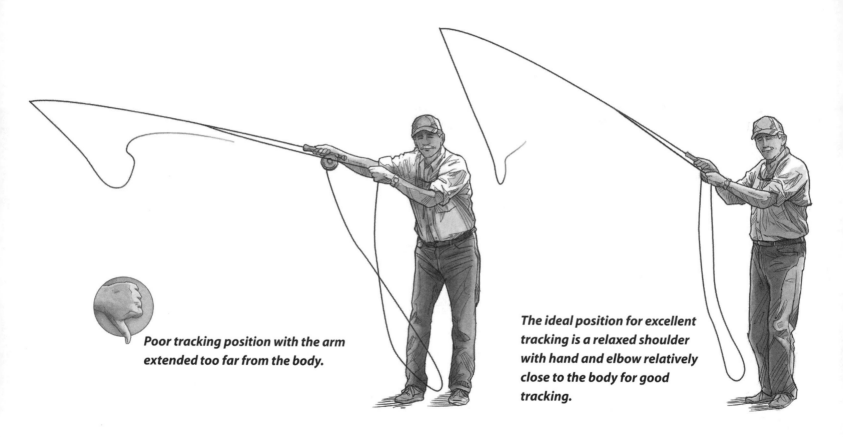

Poor tracking position with the arm extended too far from the body.

The ideal position for excellent tracking is a relaxed shoulder with hand and elbow relatively close to the body for good tracking.

A straight line at the completion of a cast is evidence of good tracking technique (left).

Following a straight-line track during the acceleration and speedup phase maximizes line control throughout the basic cast. Therefore, vigilant tracking is key to improving accuracy and distance. Since the line follows the direction of the rod tip during the casting stroke, anything other than straight-line tracking may end in an inaccurate presentation. In addition, throwing a long line with a tight loop is easier when the rod is properly loaded, without the uncontrolled slack that a curved stroke creates. As a result, casting under windy conditions with big or heavy, wind-resistant flies becomes simpler as well.

A curved line indicates an elliptical path (right).

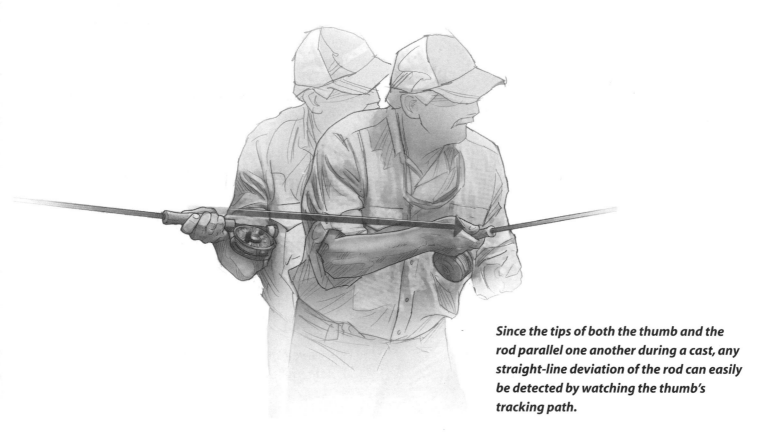

Since the tips of both the thumb and the rod parallel one another during a cast, any straight-line deviation of the rod can easily be detected by watching the thumb's tracking path.

five

The Pickup

IN MOST FISHING situations, you must lift, or pick up, a sometimes lengthy portion of fly line from the water in order to initiate a backcast. Although the pickup is an integral part of the basic overhead cast and has many of the same elements (including the acceleration and speedup phase, the stop, the straight line, loading the rod, the drop, and elimination of slack), it nevertheless has its own distinct motion. Consequently, the pickup portion of the cast deserves its own chapter.

Before initiating the pickup, you must attend to several details. First, lean slightly forward with the hand and arm extended in front of the body and the shoulders facing slightly forward at an angle almost perpendicular to the fly line. Extending the arm forward gives it a wider range of motion that provides for a longer stroke, which in turn makes it easier to pick up a lengthy section of line.

Second, since the rod will not begin to load until the terminal end of the fly line moves, it is imperative that *all* slack be stripped in before the cast is initiated. In addition, there should be no line sag between the line hand and the first stripper guide. Ideally, the rod tip should be positioned just barely above the water and pointed at the fly so that the leader, fly line, and rod are aligned. Sometimes current, wind, or other variables can make it difficult to maintain this alignment, but in a perfect scenario, the fly is immediately set in motion the moment you begin the pickup.

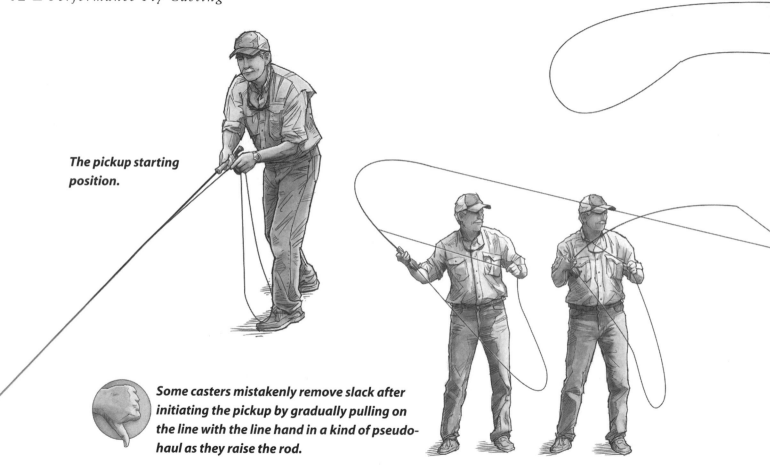

The pickup starting position.

Some casters mistakenly remove slack after initiating the pickup by gradually pulling on the line with the line hand in a kind of pseudo-haul as they raise the rod.

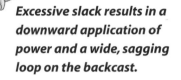

Excessive slack results in a downward application of power and a wide, sagging loop on the backcast.

Despite this simple concept, I am amazed at how many experienced fly fishers neglect to practice it.

Failure to eliminate all slack prior to the beginning of the pickup will lead to a number of problems that are further compounded as the cast progresses. Some casters mistakenly remove slack *after* initiating the pickup by gradually pulling on the line with the line hand in a kind of pseudo-haul as they raise the rod. In the worst instances, by the time the rod comes back far enough to remove slack from the line, the tip may be forced to make an inefficient downward application of power, which results in a wide, sagging loop that may even slap the water on the backcast. Such a poorly executed backcast will likewise lead to an inefficient forward stroke.

The slide-and-lift:
The fly is the only thing left
on the water when both the
haul and speedup are
simultaneously executed
(inset).

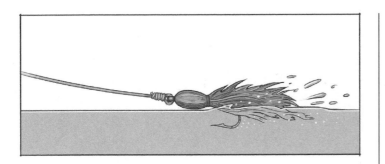

To perform a fundamentally sound pickup, you must simultaneously slide and lift the line from the water surface at an accelerated rate. The speed of this slide-and-lift motion should be fast enough that the fly line forms a straight line between the rod tip and the line's contact point with the water. For additional torque, rotate the shoulders slightly as you lift and bring the rod back. The brief speedup should occur precisely when the entire fly line has been completely picked up off the water, so that the fly is all that remains in contact with the surface. The speedup should be simultaneously accompanied by a sharp haul (see Chapter 6). After the acceleration and speedup phase, a firm stop forms the backcast loop. The slide-and-lift motion silently frees the line from water tension without leaving any surface distur-

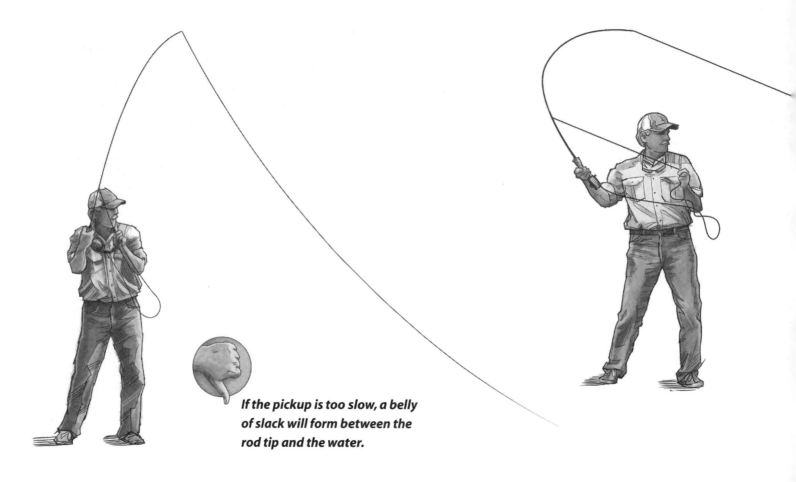

If the pickup is too slow, a belly of slack will form between the rod tip and the water.

bance that might scare fish. It also helps the rod load optimally so that you can generate superior line speed as needed for exceptionally long casts.

If the pickup is too slow, a belly of slack forms between the rod tip and the surface as the line is lifted from the water. This does not allow the rod to load sufficiently for a good backcast. On the other hand, fiercely yanking line from the water will bend the rod excessively and cause shock waves to form in the loop on the backcast. Furthermore, the surface disturbance created by jerking the rod may scare any nearby gamefish.

Yanking line off the water excessively bends the rod, creates shock waves in the line, and scares fish.

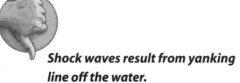

Shock waves result from yanking line off the water.

The principle that the rod tip moves in a straight line must be modified slightly for the pickup. Since the rod tip should be positioned barely above the water surface before the pickup is initiated, the straight-line path must be executed diagonally to form a nicely shaped loop on the back-cast. When a high backcast is desired, the diagonal will be steeper than it is for a lower one. After the backcast is completed, the forward stroke should be executed in the usual, more horizontal line. The combined linear paths of the pickup and forward cast resemble a V lying on its side.

The combined linear paths of the pickup and the forward cast resemble a V lying on its side.

six

The Double Haul

THE DOUBLE HAUL MAY be the least understood element of fly casting. Briefly described, a haul is made by the line hand pulling sharply downward in the direction opposite the fly-line tension during the speedup-and-turnover segment of the casting stroke. When performed properly, it is a highly effective casting tool that increases the bend or load of the rod and thereby boosts line speed. If you haul only on either the forward cast or backcast, this is referred to as a single haul, whereas pulling the line during both strokes is a double haul. Although a single haul is certainly better than no haul at all, every fly fisher should strive to make the double haul an integral part of his or her cast. With effective hauls, wind, large or heavy flies, and long casts are far less problematic, and casting in general is easier and smoother.

Mastering the Casting Stroke

In order to establish an effective double haul, you must first master the casting stroke. Too many fly fishers try to integrate the double haul into a deficient cast. But the double haul cannot compensate for inefficient casting technique. Nothing can. In fact, the double haul can make an inferior stroke even worse. I cannot overemphasize that a fundamentally sound casting stroke is a prerequisite to the proper execution of a double haul.

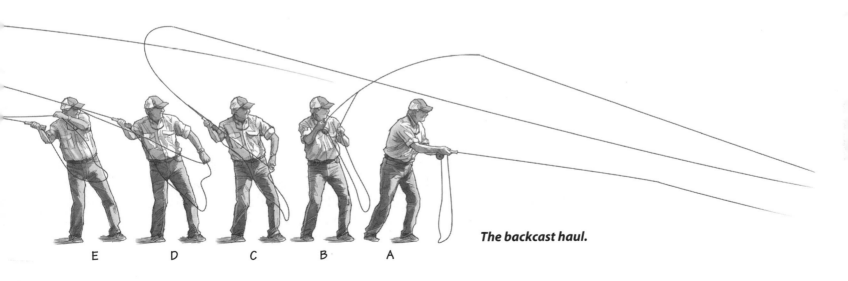

The backcast haul.

E   D   C   B   A

Executing the Double Haul

Even with a sound stroke, mastering the double haul is a common stumbling block to performance casting. Casting and hauling in synchronization is a lot like patting your head and rubbing your stomach at the same time. Consequently, a strong sense of timing is required so that the line hand and rod hand each can simultaneously perform a separate task. Because the principles of the haul are the same on both the forward and back strokes, the following explanation is applicable to all casts whenever a double haul is involved.

For the most efficient hauling, I recommend using an "in-line" position, with the hands, rod, and fly line aligned throughout the casting stroke, whether you're casting sidearm, overhead, or somewhere in between. In-line casting minimizes line friction and allows the line to easily slide through the guides in a straight line during each haul for smooth, easy casting. In comparison, holding the line at a more of an angle to the rod will increase friction through the guides and may cause the line to continuously rub against the rod in the worst instances.

When you start to accelerate the rod at the beginning of a cast, your hands should be within close proximity of one another, usually a few inches apart, with the line hand slightly below the rod hand (see position A on the illustrations on pages 81 and 83). Maintain tension on, and thereby contact with, the entire fly line by pulling on it with the line hand ever so slightly, almost imperceptibly, while accelerating the rod. Increasing the bend in the rod during this part of the casting stroke is important, but there should

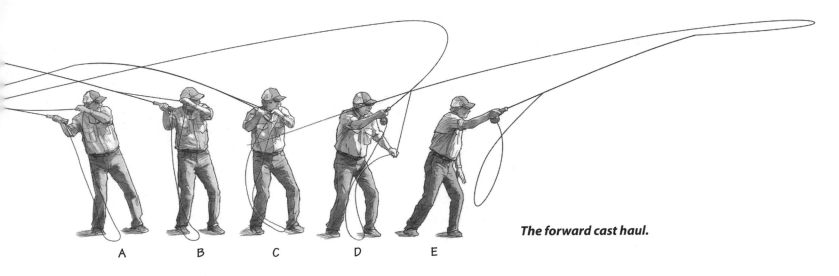

The forward cast haul.

A   B   C   D   E

be no significant separation of the hands yet. They should remain close together throughout the entire acceleration phase.

As you seamlessly transition from the acceleration part of the stroke and begin the brief speedup and turnover, start the haul by pulling on the line at an angle that is in alignment with the rod to maintain the in-line position. (See position B on page 81 and C on page 83.)

Because the haul and the speedup-and-turnover motion occur at the same time, it is imperative that they be synchronized to start and finish together. Therefore, the haul should cease the moment the rod is stopped at the completion of the casting stroke. (See position C on page 81 and D on page 83.)

In executing the haul, don't abruptly yank on the line, as this would shock the rod and create waves of slack in the

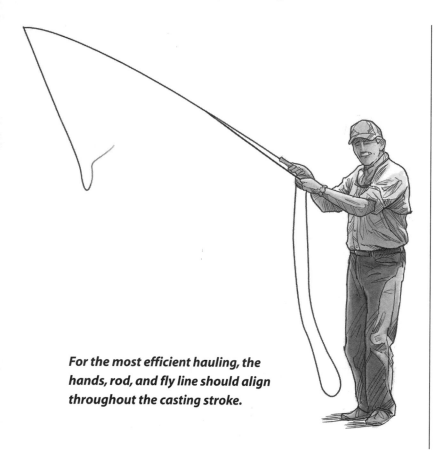

For the most efficient hauling, the hands, rod, and fly line should align throughout the casting stroke.

loop. Likewise, avoid pulling at an even speed. Instead, haul on the line at an increasingly rapid rate so that maximum speed is achieved precisely when the stroke and haul concurrently end. (See position D on page 81 and E on page 83.)

Haul Length and Speed

There is no set haul length or speed. These factors vary slightly from one cast to another. However, the speed and length of the haul should exactly reflect or mimic these same qualities in the speedup, since both take place simultaneously. Whether the speedup segment is fast, slow, long, or short, it should be accompanied by a haul that has these same qualities. For example, a speedup that is short and quick should be accompanied by a haul of proportionate length and speed.

Shooting Line

Immediately following the completion of the casting stroke and haul, you will feel the momentum of the unrolling fly line start to pull on the line hand slightly—*if* the haul and cast have been properly executed. At that moment, you can release or "shoot" line by simply relaxing your grip so that the line slides loosely between thumb and fingers.

To add line on either the forward or back stroke when false-casting, continue to let the line slide through the fingers. At the same time, allow the line hand to move in conjunction with the ascending pull of the line until it has gravitated to its original starting position just below and within a few inches of the rod hand. This principle that *the line hand always returns to the rod hand* is essential to high-performance hauling and is a continuation of the in-line process. Furthermore, the line hand must return all the way to the rod hand before the next consecutive stroke is started, or unwanted slack will develop. (See position E on page 81.)

While the line is still shooting, and just before the loop has time to completely unroll, grasp the line firmly again and wait or watch for the rod tip to bend slightly under the weight of the fly line; if the line straightens or the rod loses its bend, you've waited too long. At that point, it's time to initiate the next forward cast or backcast, as the case may be. Using the same technique, continue to work out additional line by false-casting until there is sufficient length and weight to shoot the fly toward its intended target.

To shoot line on either the forward or back stroke when false casting. Note that the line hand always returns to the rod hand.

The water haul.

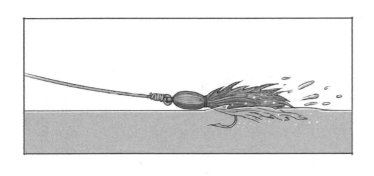

Double Haul Practice

The best way to perfect the double haul is to use it in conjunction with the ground stroke (Chapter 9). This reduces the cast and haul to their most basic elements, significantly improving the learning curve. Once you have perfected the double haul via ground stroke practice, it is easy to incorporate it into an aerialized cast.

The Water Haul

When trying to execute a pickup (refer to Chapter 5), the line should be lifted smoothly off the water as it is accelerated during the initial backward motion of the rod. Once the fly is the *only* thing remaining on the water and the rod has been sufficiently loaded, the speedup portion of the backcast can be executed simultaneously with a haul. This water haul results in an exceptionally quiet pickup and a backcast with the kind of speed that makes it easy to shoot the line an incredible distance on the following forward stroke.

seven

Relaxed Casting

CASTING A SMOOTH AND ripple-free loop is an integral part of performance fly casting. However, even an experienced caster can instinctively tighten up under pressure to increase distance, speed up the delivery, or make a particularly difficult presentation. The result of this tension, more often than not, is an inefficient cast.

Ideally, proficient casting should look effortless, with neat loops and a smooth line at all distances; however, some fly fishers appear to strain whenever they make a cast. Relaxed casting not only is more efficient, but also involves considerably less work than a more tense style. Fly fishers who seem to work the hardest probably do—and they get

tired in the process. Outside of good casting mechanics, a relaxed stroke may be the most crucial factor in developing an efficient stroke. Relaxing doesn't imply that effort is not exerted, only that the cast appears effortless. Even some otherwise fundamentally sound casters could improve their strokes by learning to relax at the right times.

Tense and rigid muscles are not conducive to fluid movement and the top performance of any sports skill— including fly casting. To stay relaxed, many great hitters in baseball move their fingers almost continuously on the bat while awaiting a pitch. Some grip the bat so loosely that it may occasionally slip out of their hands as they take a swing. Similarly, professional golfers are not rigid while addressing the ball, nor do they hold the club with a white-knuckle grip. Both golfers and baseball players rely on a relaxed, smooth, and fundamentally sound swing while avoiding the futile urge to "kill" the ball—a move that usually yields poor results. Similarly, the desire to be forceful with the rod usually ends badly. Furthermore, tight muscles can lead to cramping and fatigue.

Although the entire body should remain relatively loose and at ease during the cast, the most important areas to focus on are the casting hand and arm. A white-knuckle "death" grip or excessively tight arm and shoulder muscles are detrimental to a smooth line, because they cause the rod to recoil and oscillate significantly after the stop at the end of both the forward and back strokes. That tightness and the associated recoil occur most often when trying to overpower the rod in order to achieve extra distance, make a good stop, and speed up the delivery. Trying to cast a long line with a compact stroke instead of a more appropriate lengthier motion can have the same effect as well. The recoil creates an inefficient loop with shock waves of undesirable slack in the line that are difficult to manage.

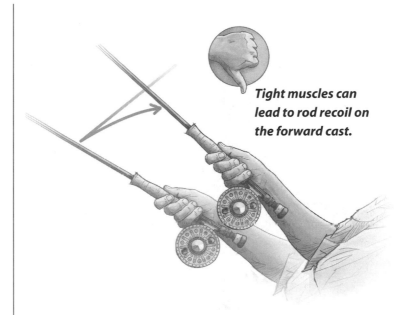

Tight muscles can lead to rod recoil on the forward cast.

As described in Chapter 3, reducing rod recoil for more fluid casting is similar to stopping a car smoothly. Unless the muscles in the casting arm and hand are relaxed during the stop (the equivalent of foot pressure being reduced on the car's brake pedal), the rod will recoil.

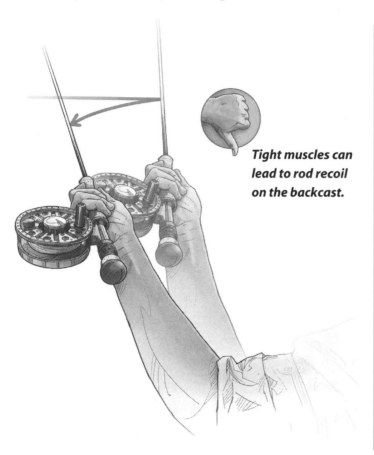

Tight muscles can lead to rod recoil on the backcast.

To reduce recoil so that the rod dampens or stabilizes for a smooth cast, your grip should be firm but not excessively tight throughout the acceleration-and-speedup segment of the casting stroke. Then, immediately after the stop, loosen the grip significantly and allow the rod to drift slightly with the line as the loop unfolds. The combination of loosened grip and drifting rod will immediately dampen the rod for a more effective stop so that the line flows smoothly through the air. You can then reestablish a firm grip each time you begin another stroke. Alternating the grip from firm to loose will substantially reduce recoil and keep the line free of any shock waves in the process.

Sometimes stiff arm muscles go hand in hand with a white-knuckle grip. Simply relaxing the casting arm along with the hand after the stop will further help dampen the rod for a smoother motion.

You can easily detect recoil by watching the line, rod tip, and rod hand after the stop at the end of each stroke. A wavy line, substantial rod-tip oscillation, and casting hand recoil indicate an excessively tight grip on the rod, muscle rigidity in the arm, or both. That same rigidity and tension can also cause you to yank the rod to a violent stop instead of fluidly accelerating to a relaxed stop. Yanking

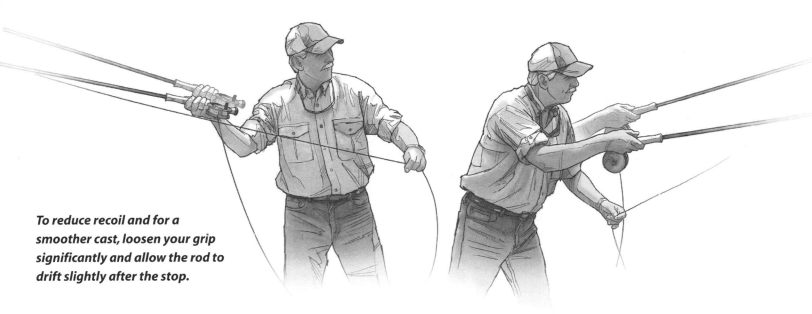

To reduce recoil and for a smoother cast, loosen your grip significantly and allow the rod to drift slightly after the stop.

occurs most frequently on the pickup, and in the worst instances, the casting hand and arm recoil so severely that the entire rod immediately snaps back to an almost vertical position.

Situations can develop quickly on the water, and you may often feel pressured to hurriedly make a presentation. Although it's important to concentrate on the fish, part of your focus must remain on smoothly loading the rod for a more relaxed, but still prompt, delivery. Tight loops, a fluid line, and increased distance become easier to achieve as well. Just don't relax so much that the rod and reel accidentally slip out of your hand in the process.

eight

Creep

SOMETIMES WHEN A speedy presentation is necessary, the natural inclination is to hurry the forward casting stroke by moving the rod before it has a chance to bend under the weight of the line. As a result, the rod doesn't load until the very end of the forward stroke, so the fly fisher loses control of the cast. For that reason, fly casters should keep in mind the following principle: hurrying the forward cast does not speed up the presentation; it will either hamper or ruin the cast.

Ideally, the rod should progressively load or bend throughout the forward stroke. However, if the forward motion begins too soon, while the line is still unrolling on the backcast, the rod and line are actually traveling in opposite directions. This premature forward motion is commonly referred to as creep, and it is sometimes accompanied by a loud snap that is reminiscent of a cracking whip. As the rod creeps forward in a quasi forward stroke, slack is removed until the line eventually straightens out behind the caster, suddenly pulling against the rod to load it. Unfortunately, by then the rod has crept so far forward that the effective length of the casting stroke has been shortened significantly by the amount of slack in the line. Consequently, the caster is left with no alternative but to make a short jab with the tip to complete the forward cast.

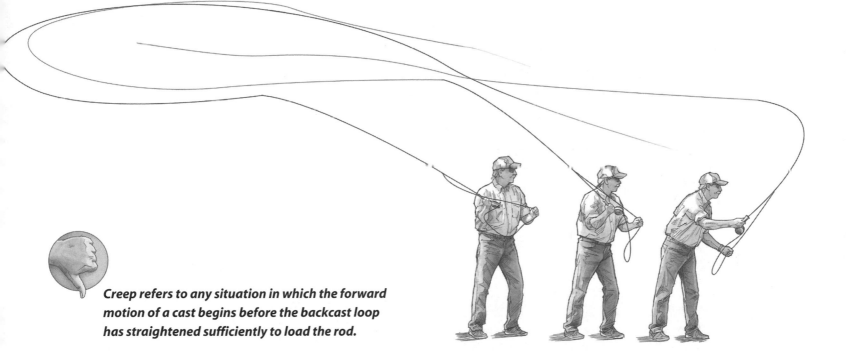

Creep refers to any situation in which the forward motion of a cast begins before the backcast loop has straightened sufficiently to load the rod.

Backcast pseudo-haul.

Creep is often accompanied by the caster pulling steadily down on the line with the line hand from the beginning of a stroke until the end in a kind of pseudo-haul to get rid of any remaining slack. Unlike a true haul, this pseudo-haul only removes slack; it does not increase the bend in the rod or speed up the line like a bona fide haul will. Furthermore, a pseudo-haul does not allow the line hand to return properly to the rod hand (refer to chaper 6).

The problem of creep is much more common than many fly fishers realize, and it can vary from being almost imperceptible to obvious. Although some anglers may creep while false-casting, it happens most frequently and severely on the final forward stroke that presents the fly to the fish. Creep is undesirable in any situation, but a fly fisher can sometimes get away with it to a small degree on short casts. However, it's a terminal problem when attempting to cast longer distances. Accuracy suffers at all distances as well. Moreover, although creep is not the cause of tailing loops, it often leads to them.

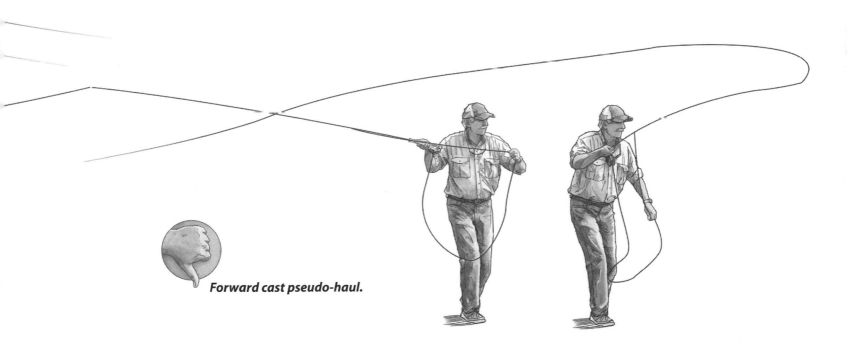

Forward cast pseudo-haul.

A sagging loop leads to creep. The unwanted slack created by a sagging or collapsed loop prevents the line from straightening, and the caster has to depend on forward creep to take up that excess line and load the rod.

Causes

Creep is a common problem for fly fishers who never develop a feel for the rod loading after the completion of the backcast. Consequently, they creep the rod forward until they detect the pull of the line as it straightens and bends the tip; however, it's only then that the casting stroke becomes effective. In extreme cases, casters don't pause at all after the backcast and instead immediately creep the rod forward so that the backcast and forward cast appear to be one continuous stroke.

Some fly fishers try to load the rod by carrying more line in the air than they are capable of straightening on the backcast. Under these circumstances, the loop will not

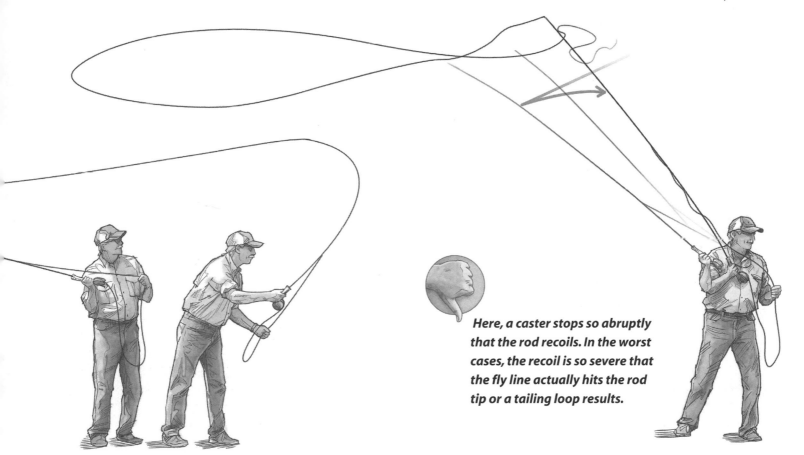

Here, a caster stops so abruptly that the rod recoils. In the worst cases, the recoil is so severe that the fly line actually hits the rod tip or a tailing loop results.

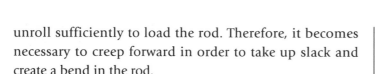

Cocking the wrist prevents the rod tip from accelerating progressively throughout the cast so that the caster must make a semi-circular motion with the tip in order to complete the forward cast.

unroll sufficiently to load the rod. Therefore, it becomes necessary to creep forward in order to take up slack and create a bend in the rod.

Several other factors induce creep, including a poorly formed loop on the backcast. When the line doesn't straighten on the backcast, the caster begins the forward cast too soon in an attempt to take up the excess line.

Another type of creep occurs when a caster stops so abruptly and rigidly on the backcast that the rod recoils partially back to a forward position. In the worst instances, the recoil is so severe that the fly line actually hits the rod tip or a tailing loop results.

In many instances, fly fishers will even cock the wrist back during the forward creep to help propel the line at the end of the stroke when they finally feel the rod load. Cocking the wrist prevents the rod tip from accelerating progressively throughout the cast. Consequently, the casters must make a semicircular motion with the tip in order to complete the forward cast. The result is a round loop in which

Some casters lean forward immediately after the stop and prior to any movement of the rod. This leads to a breaking or cocking of the wrist and the subsequent rounded loop.

the fly either strikes (a tailing loop) or almost touches the fly line. On occasion, the fly may even hit the rod tip.

Instead of slightly shifting the body weight in unison with the rod's forward motion, some casters lean forward immediately after the stop and prior to any movement of the rod. This leads to a breaking or cocking of the wrist and the subsequent rounded loop.

Frequently, when circumstances call for a quick presentation, a fly fisher's impatience or excitement can lead to creep and the resultant inefficient cast. The situation is

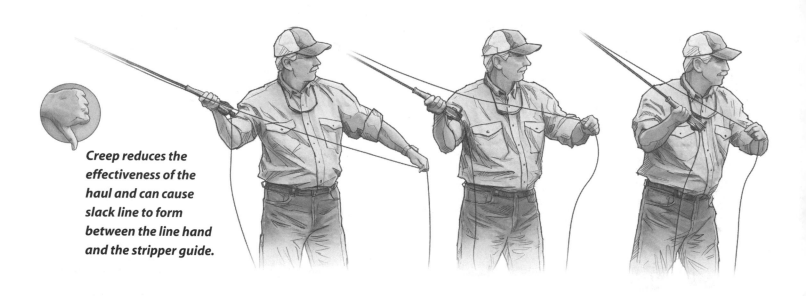

Creep reduces the effectiveness of the haul and can cause slack line to form between the line hand and the stripper guide.

roughly the equivalent of a hunter's "buck fever." As an example, I've seen accomplished trout anglers experience a casting meltdown because of premature forward rod motion during their initial attempts at making a speedy presentation to saltwater gamefish whose transient nature seems to keep them on the move.

Creep will reduce the effectiveness of the haul and can even render it useless because it does not allow sufficient time for the line hand to return to the rod hand.

Solutions

Watching the rod tip is an easy way to reveal a creeping movement. Ideally, the rod should maintain a bend throughout the forward cast, and no recoil should be evident after the back stop. Another indication of creep is lack of sufficient pause that allows the loop to unfold on the backcast.

A large part of the solution to creep is rather simple:

- Relax.
- Concentrate on forming good loops.
- Lengthen your casting stroke.
- Slow down a bit.
- Don't aerialize more line than you can straighten on the backcast.
- Shift your body weight, without rocking, in conjunction with the forward movement of the rod.
- Always wait for the rod to load or watch for the tip to bend before starting the forward cast.
- Practice the line-hand-to-rod-hand principle when double hauling.
- Let the rod drift back slowly while the line unrolls on the backcast. A well-executed drift is similar to creep, except the angler moves the rod in the opposite direction; think of it as reverse creep.

Once you've eliminated any creep from your casting stroke, you can feel more confident about making high-performance casts.

nine

The Ground Stroke

THE BEST CASTERS REGULARLY reserve time to hone their skills, but even the casual fly fisher should set aside practice periods separate from times spent chasing fish. When it comes to helping beginning and experienced fly fishers alike develop a fundamentally sound cast, I am a strong advocate of what I refer to as the ground stroke, a term that derives its name from the fact that it is a land-based practice technique with no water involved. I believe that practicing the ground stroke is the easiest and best way to learn to fly-cast and have also found that it can help solve more casting problems than any other corrective measure; however, a thorough understanding of the elements and fundamental principles of a properly executed cast (as described in this text) is essential for the ground stroke to be used effectively. Otherwise, practicing poor techniques will result in perfecting bad habits.

Problems can be difficult to rectify when the line remains in the air throughout the entire cast, because this doesn't allow enough time to analyze the elements of each stroke. In contrast, those same mistakes are easier to identify and technique is more readily modified through ground strokes. With this procedure, you let the line lie on the ground after each backcast or forward cast, while you take the time necessary to analyze the mechanics of one stroke separately from the other instead of having to consider both strokes together. Keep this book at hand as a reference while practicing the principles and elements in each chapter.

To begin, stretch a manageable amount of line in front of you; somewhere between 20 and 60 feet is a good length, as long as it is free of slack and not difficult to control. Never use more line than you can easily straighten out on either the fore or back strokes. Assume a standard open stance that is roughly parallel to the direction you'll be casting. Using a thumb-on-top grip, hold the rod slightly above horizontal (up to a maximum 45-degree angle) for the clearest view of the rod tip and fly line, which are reference points for examining the characteristics of each stroke and its resultant loop. Holding the rod vertically for an overhead cast doesn't work well with the ground stroke.

To execute a good backcast, start with the rod hand extended in front of you with the rod tip pointing forward and to the side at about head or eye height. A long line requires a longer stroke than a shorter length of line, so the distance the hand and rod are extended before the cast is initiated depends on the amount of fly line lying on the ground in front of you. For 20 to 30 feet of line, use the same starting position as illustrated on page 104. A longer length up to 60 feet will require that the arm and hand be fully extended forward at the start.

Using the index finger for leverage (refer to Chapter 2), begin dragging the line slowly along the ground, gradually and smoothly increasing speed so that the rod bends ever deeper as the stroke progresses. The tip must accelerate in a straight line that is parallel to the ground. Try to imagine drawing a straight line with the rod tip or visually align it with a building's roof line or some other horizontal reference point. Unless you are also practicing the double haul, keep the rod hand and line hand equidistant from one another so that there is no significant separation of the two throughout either the back or forward ground stroke. You can also opt to execute the ground stroke by holding the line and rod in the same hand.

Continue the rod's rearward acceleration until it is time to shift the rod tip position from pointing slightly forward to pointing rearward. The speedup occurs precisely during this directional shift, or turnover, as it is sometimes called. To complete the speedup and turnover, quicken the rate of

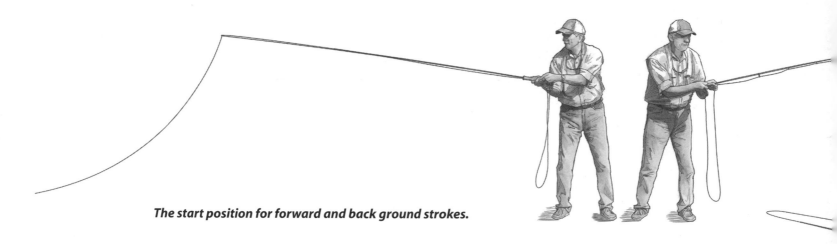

The start position for forward and back ground strokes.

acceleration at the very end of the stroke, and then stop the rod firmly while still maintaining a straight line. The transition from acceleration to speedup should be seamless and not two distinct segments.

In executing the backcast, the hand and elbow both move rearward during the acceleration and speedup phase, but the hand should extend past the elbow by the completion of the stroke. The longer the line being cast, the greater the extension should be. Again, keep in mind that the

length of the casting stroke must increase proportionately with the length of line. Relax your grip on the rod after the stop so that the line unrolls smoothly.

After the line has come to rest on the ground, take time to analyze the results, based on the information in the previous chapters, and make any necessary modifications in your technique. This is one of the great advantages of the ground stroke: it allows you sufficient time to consider one stroke separately from the other. Begin the forward ground stroke only after you've thoroughly examined and analyzed the backcast.

The forward motion is executed in the same manner as the backcast. Start the forward stroke with the rod positioned rearward and the tip about head or eye height. The hand should be extended past the elbow (in the same position as at the end of the back stroke); the longer the line, the farther the extension. (See the illustration on page 104.) Holding the rod primarily with the bottom three fingers and pushing forward with the thumb for leverage, slide the

Backcast speedup and turnover.

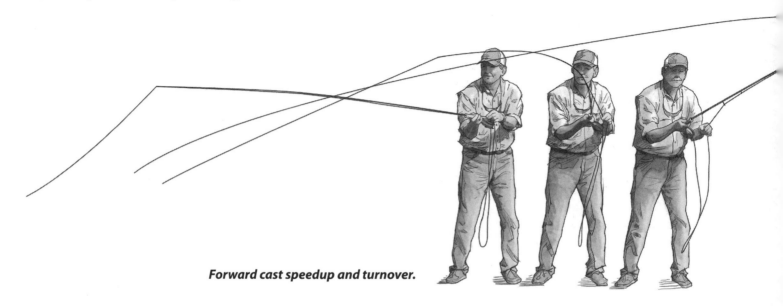

Forward cast speedup and turnover.

line along the ground at an accelerated rate while maintaining a straight line with the rod tip. Proceed with the forward motion of the rod, hand, and elbow until it's time for the tip to transition from pointing slightly rearward to pointing forward.

It is during this turnover that the speedup occurs, with the rod tip reaching peak acceleration immediately prior to the stop that completes the stroke. Allow the line to unroll on the ground, and then take time to analyze the forward stroke the same way you did the backcast.

Once the results of the ground strokes are satisfactory, it's time to aerialize the cast by simply using the same exact back and forward motions, but without allowing the line to touch the ground. To allow sufficient time for the rod to load properly after each stop, watch the rod tip and wait for it to bend under the load of the weighted line before initiating each successive stroke. Avoid creeping forward as the line straightens.

It really isn't necessary to execute the drop phase at the end of the forward ground stroke. You can choose to include or exclude it at your own discretion. However, if you are a beginning or relatively inexperienced fly caster, it will be easier and you will have less to worry about if you end the forward ground stroke with the rod tip at head or

Experienced casters will want to incorporate the drop into their ground stroke so that it becomes instinctive at the end of any aerialized cast.

eye height instead of lowering it at the completion of each cast. On the other hand, more experienced casters should incorporate the drop into their ground stoke practice so that it becomes instinctive at the end of any aerialized cast. The drop must also be integrated into the ground stroke in order to perfect the slide-and-lift portion of the pickup (refer to Chapter 5).

As an aid in developing good loops and maintaining a straight line path, try performing the ground stroke by casting sidearm while on your knees or in a crouched position. Keep the loop as close to the ground as possible without allowing it to touch until the end of each stroke. Think of the line as being a giant weed whacker barely clipping the tops of the grass. Not only will this technique help you create better loops, but it also will develop your skill for casting under overhanging vegetation in the process.

The ground stroke is also an excellent means for learning or improving the double haul. Refer to Chapter 6 when introducing the haul into ground stroke practice.

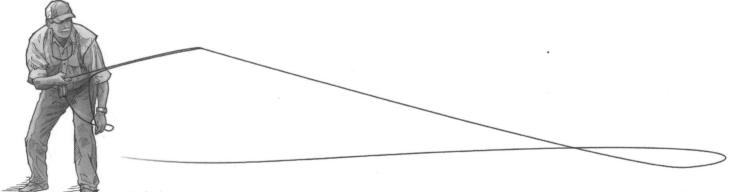

To help maintain a straight line path and develop good loops, incorporate the weed-whacker technique into your ground stroke practice.

ten

Casting in Windy Conditions

MORE OFTEN THAN NOT wind is a factor during our fly-fishing forays. Although we fly fishers tend to complain, the wind isn't always our nemesis. In fact, it can even be the precursor to great fishing, as it sometimes makes fish less uneasy than in calmer conditions. However, casting deficiencies are quickly magnified in wind.

Some anglers simply resort to staying at home when they deem it too windy, while others reach for spinning or plug gear. But short of gale force conditions, there's no reason to put away the fly rod. With a few simple adjustments, anyone can continue to enjoy time on the water regardless of whether there's a strong head-, tail-, or crosswind.

Headwind

Any presentation directly into a headwind can be challenging. Some fly fishers try to force the line into an advancing breeze by overpowering the cast. This causes them to extend their arm too far forward and simultaneously drop the rod

109

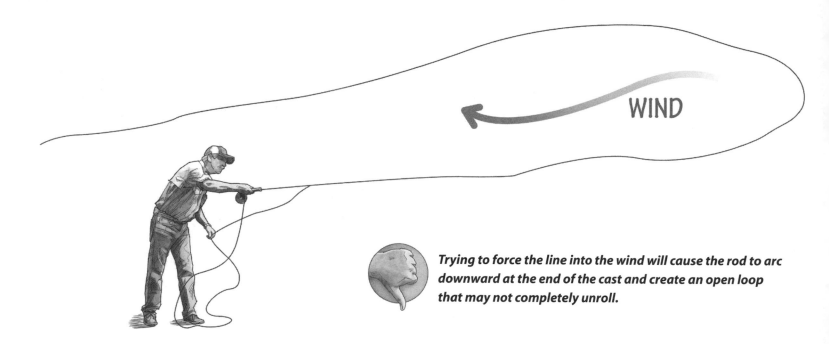

WIND

Trying to force the line into the wind will cause the rod to arc downward at the end of the cast and create an open loop that may not completely unroll.

in a wide, downward arc without making a firm stop—the single most important element of any cast. The result is a wide, irregularly shaped loop that presents a large exposed surface area lacking sufficient energy to unroll against the wind. Firm stops, tight loops, and the elimination of slack are fundamental to almost any good presentation, but these factors become increasingly important as wind velocity increases. A sharp haul in combination with fluid accelera-

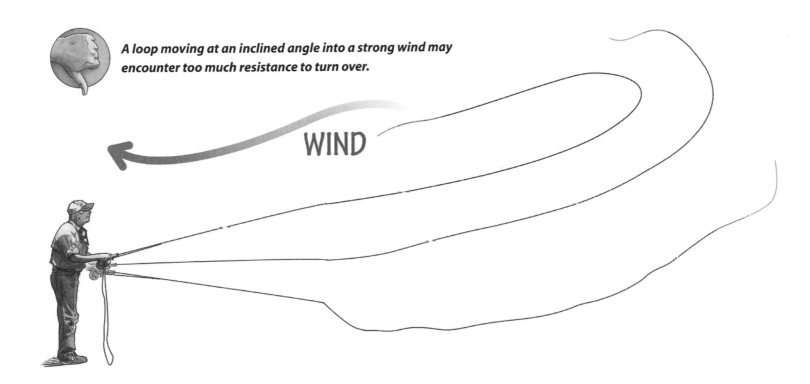

A loop moving at an inclined angle into a strong wind may encounter too much resistance to turn over.

WIND

tion, a quick speedup, and a firm stop will tighten the loop and build enough line speed for penetration.

Loop angle is another primary consideration when casting into a headwind. Under ordinary conditions, an ideal loop either parallels the water surface or tilts slightly above horizontal on the forward cast. However, because air currents normally move horizontally, any loop parallel to a stiff breeze may encounter too much resistance to turn over.

A loop moving at an inclined angle into a strong wind will meet with significant resistance as well.

Against a strong headwind, the best path for a loop to follow is a slightly downward angle to the horizontal air current, so that the loop is aimed at the target. To accomplish this, first make a backcast loop that is tilted slightly upward. Since the rod tip should travel in a straight line, the angle of the backcast should be directly opposite (180 degrees) the anticipated downward diagonal you'll make on the forward stroke. In conjunction with a snappy haul, a sig-

Against a strong headwind, the best path for a loop is at a slight downward angle to the horizontal air current.

nificant acceleration-and-speedup phase, and a firm stop, the downward momentum of the loop on the forward cast will help turn the line and fly over. These angled casts are easiest to achieve using a mostly sidearm or three-quarters casting motion.

Tailwind

The same principles used to battle a headwind also pertain to a tailwind. A low backcast with a tight, wind-resistant loop angled beneath the tailwind offers the best penetration. I prefer to use a slightly sidearm motion for the backcast, and then bring the rod a little more overhead on the forward stroke so that I can angle the loop just above the horizontal plane and thereby take advantage of the tailwind to push the loop downwind for extra distance (as needed) as well as a good turnover. In this case, opening the loop a little on the forward stroke offers more surface area against which the wind can push.

Crosswind

In a crosswind, accuracy becomes more difficult to achieve as wind speed increases. To improve accuracy, aim the loop horizontally, and then immediately lower your rod tip and line to the water after the stop so that the line has little chance to blow sideways as it unrolls. Although this technique improves accuracy, it does not lend itself to shooting

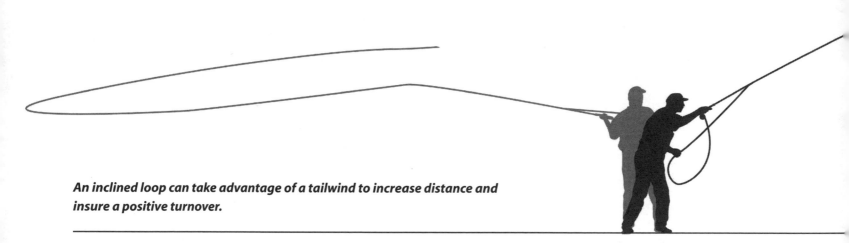

***An inclined loop can take advantage of a tailwind to increase distance and
insure a positive turnover.***

a lot of line. Consequently, you must be able to aerialize
most of the line needed to reach the intended target.

When you must shoot line, your only option is to rely
on instinct to estimate how far the wind will blow the cast
off-target, and then compensate by aiming at some point
upwind. If time and circumstances allow, an extra false cast
or two lets you better gauge wind drift for a more accurate
presentation.

A crosswind blowing into your line-hand side (the left
side of a right-handed caster) is relatively easy to deal with,

but wind from your casting side (the right side of a right-handed caster) presents a more difficult situation, as the line or fly could conceivably hit you or the rod. Some individuals try to adjust to the problem by either holding the rod as far windward as possible or making a backhand cast over the opposite shoulder. Both of these methods are ineffective for anything but the shortest casts.

There are several better ways to deal with wind blowing toward your rod hand. Ambidextrous fly fishers simply

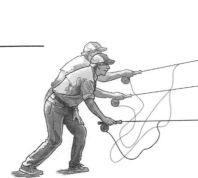

To increase accuracy in a crosswind, immediately lower the rod tip to the water after the loop is formed.

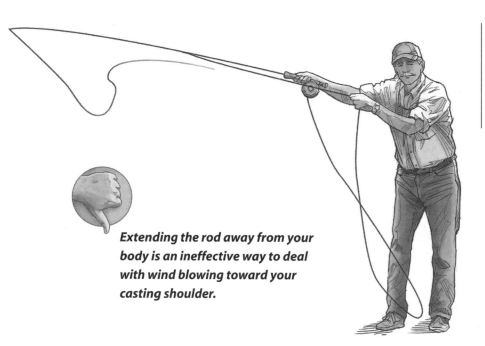

switch the rod hand. Others prefer to turn around 180 degrees and then, with the rod hand thereby moved to the leeward side of the body, use a backcast to make the presentation. This second method is extremely effective for casters with fundamentally sound technique, but those

Extending the rod away from your body is an ineffective way to deal with wind blowing toward your casting shoulder.

Except for short presentations, a backhand cast is inefficient for dealing with a crosswind blowing toward your casting shoulder.

who drop the tip without making a firm stop or fail to track the rod in a straight line end up with inaccurate casts and open loops that will not turn over.

Another effective way to keep the line from hitting you or the rod is to make simple modifications to the basic casting stroke. To begin, slant the rod off to the side at about a 45-degree angle in order to keep the line on the windward side during the backcast. Then, while the line straightens after the back stroke, tilt the rod tip just slightly past vertical to the downwind side so that the line and fly pass safely to leeward during the forward stroke. This cast is relatively easy to accomplish, but it requires a leap of faith for skeptics.

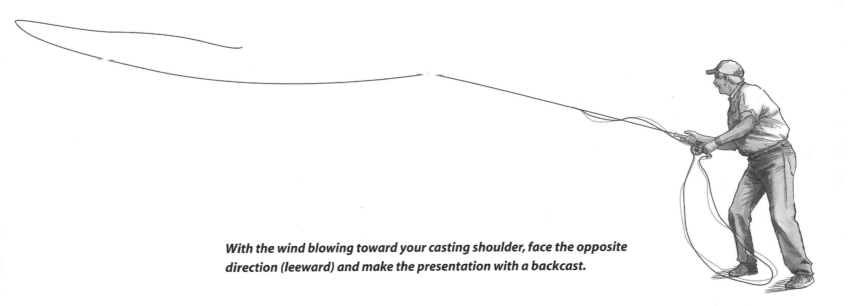

With the wind blowing toward your casting shoulder, face the opposite direction (leeward) and make the presentation with a backcast.

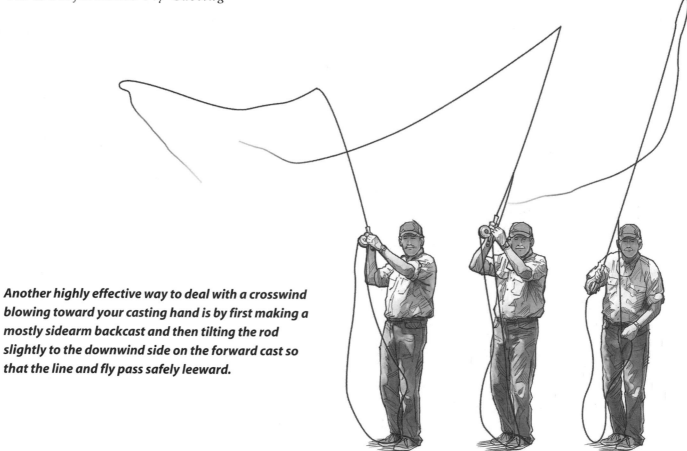

Another highly effective way to deal with a crosswind blowing toward your casting hand is by first making a mostly sidearm backcast and then tilting the rod slightly to the downwind side on the forward cast so that the line and fly pass safely leeward.

Additional Tips for Dealing with Wind

- If conditions permit, change to a higher-density line, such as from a floating line to an intermediate one. Because of their smaller diameter, sinking lines are less wind-resistant and therefore easier to cast in wind than floating lines.
- Try a fly line with a blunt forward taper, which may facilitate casting into wind.
- Use a short, heavy leader, which will turn over more easily in windy conditions than a long, light leader.
- Switch to a smaller, more streamlined fly.
- When circumstances allow, move to a more strategically located casting position with regard to the wind rather than try to make a difficult presentation that has little chance of success.
- In a strong breeze, avoid uplining the rod, because the added weight and larger diameter of a heavier line will cause the rod to bend more deeply when loaded, creating bigger, more wind-resistant loops. A better solution is to downline by one line weight. The smaller diameter is less wind-resistant, and the reduction in weight will allow you to carry more line outside the tip with tight loops.
- During the initial backcast and any subsequent false casts, make sure the loop has enough momentum to turn over, or the resulting slack will destroy the presentation. In wind, it is often necessary to keep less line outside the rod tip than under calmer conditions.

eleven

The Speed Cast

SALTWATER GAMEFISH SEEM to always be on the move, whereas freshwater species tend to be more settled and generally prefer to remain in a particular area. As a result, there's usually sufficient time to reflect on each set of circumstances before making a cast in streams and lakes, whereas you must be ready and able to react instantaneously in marine environments.

Whether you are sight-fishing the flats or casting to fish sporadically emerging from deep water to chase bait on the surface, the ability to quickly make an accurate and frequently long presentation is vital to your consistent success in salt water. Once you spot a marine gamefish, the passage of time immediately becomes the enemy, as you usually will have only precious few moments in which to deliver a fly. Seconds wasted on excessive false casting can suddenly turn a promising situation into a lost cause. Consequently, any marine fly fishers worth their salt must master some variation of the speed cast regardless of whether they fish from a boat or wade.

The object of a speed cast is to expedite the presentation by reducing the number of false casts. This is largely accomplished by extending a long but manageable length of fly line outside the rod tip in preparation for making a cast. The longer the length, and thus greater the weight, the better the rod loads during the initial false cast, which in turn facilitates shooting additional line on each progressive

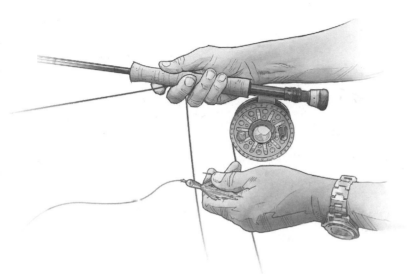

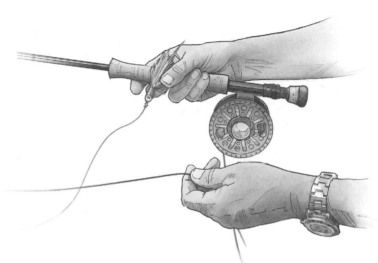

Ready position for a speed cast (option 1):
Grasp the fly in your line hand while you tuck the
line underneath either your index or middle finger.

Ready position for a speed cast
(option 2): Hold the fly in the rod
hand and the line in the line hand.

back and forward stroke until there is enough line to carry the fly to the fish.

There are several variations of the speed cast. Before beginning any of them, you must strip all the line you'll need from the reel, making sure that the length will easily reach the maximum intended casting distance. You never want to come up short. To avoid entanglements, first cast the line, and then strip it back into an orderly pile so that the rear portion of line is on the bottom of the accumulation and the front section sits on top.

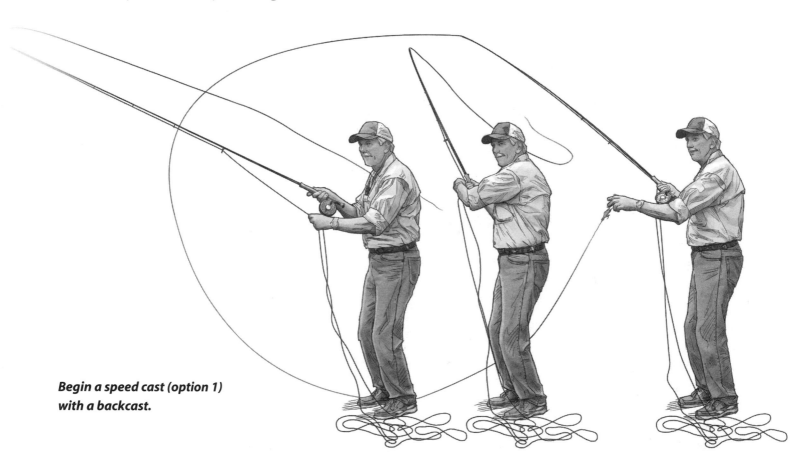

Begin a speed cast (option 1) with a backcast.

With a standard speed cast, you must stand ready with the leader and about 10 to 12 feet of fly line outside the rod tip and the fly held in either the casting hand or line hand. If you use the line hand, grasp the fly between the thumb and index finger of this hand while tucking the line under the index or middle finger of the rod hand. A minor drawback to this method is the slight possibility that you may encounter some difficulty in transferring the line from the rod hand to the line hand once the cast is under way and the fly has been released. If problems develop, secure the fly between the thumb and first or second fingers of the rod hand while clutching the line normally with the other hand. Whatever method you employ, grip the fly by either the rear tips of the tying material or the hook bend.

Begin a speed cast (option 2) with a roll pickup.

From this ready position, you have two options for beginning a speed cast. The first starts with the rod pointed at the intended target to ensure accuracy, after which the speed cast is initiated with a backcast. In contrast, the second alternative is initiated with a roll pickup, which is then followed by a backcast. When using option two, it is critical that the roll pickup tracks toward the target in order to ensure a good backcast, provide accuracy, and eliminate slack. With either method, you must wait for the momentum of the moving line to pull the fly from between your fingers in order to help load the rod. The fly should not be thrown into the air or otherwise released prematurely, as the resulting slack will fail to load the rod adequately. The idea is to feed out as much line as necessary using the fewest number of false casts in order to reach a fish. The quickest presentation can be accomplished only by shooting line on both the backcast and forward cast.

False casting can be further reduced for a faster presentation by adding to the length of line held outside the rod tip, but as that length increases, line management becomes more difficult. To control up to about 20 feet of line outside the tip requires preparation that is slightly more compli-

cated than with a standard speed cast. The fly must be held between the thumb and index finger of the line hand. From a point about 5 feet from the front end of the fly line, lay the line loosely across the remaining three fingers. Hold the standing end of the line against the cork grip with either of the first two fingers; using the middle finger will raise the line away from the grip, where it becomes easier to grasp when transferred to the line hand.

My favorite way to reach maximum distance with the fewest false casts is to trail a long loop of line off to the lee side and behind me in the water. After a fish is sighted, I execute a roll pickup cast to get the trailing loop into the air and pull the fly free from the line hand. The resistance of the water against the relatively lengthy section of line sufficiently loads the rod so that a fair amount of line can be shot on the roll pickup and corresponding backcast.

In many instances, it is possible to reach a considerable distance with only one false cast if there is enough line outside the tip from the outset. However, trailing a large amount of line is not without its drawbacks. If the trailing loop is too long when fishing from a boat, the line may tangle around the propeller, a pushpole, a trolling motor, or some other appurtenance on the vessel that projects into the water. Furthermore, because the trailing loop of line can collect dead sea grass or catch on protruding vegetation and structure, you have to monitor the line constantly and reposition it whenever it encounters these or other impediments. Maintaining a grip on the fly and then making a roll cast will clean off dead grass, and this same procedure can be used to flip the line over protrusions. However, this method becomes impractical where flotsam and structure are so thick as to require constant monitoring.

Sometimes after making a presentation to a fish, you may strip in so much line that not enough remains outside the rod tip to recast promptly. For example, a fish may follow a fly for such a considerable distance without striking that very little line is left in the water. To quickly get more line outside the tip in order to make another speedy delivery, release line through the fingers while raising the rod slowly for the pickup. The extra line can be combined with a water haul to immediately get the fly back in action.

At times it may become necessary to quickly decrease the length of line in order to make a short cast. This is

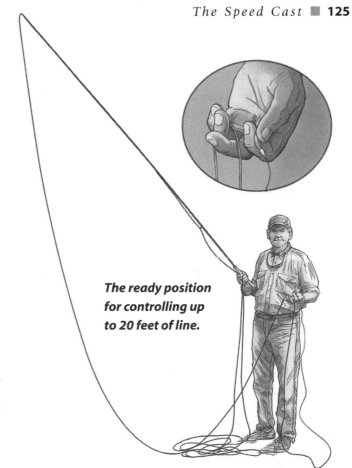

The ready position for controlling up to 20 feet of line.

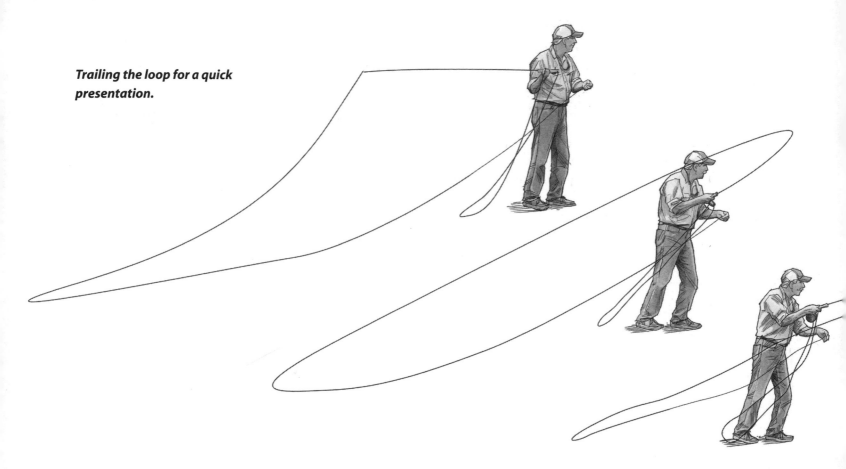

Trailing the loop for a quick presentation.

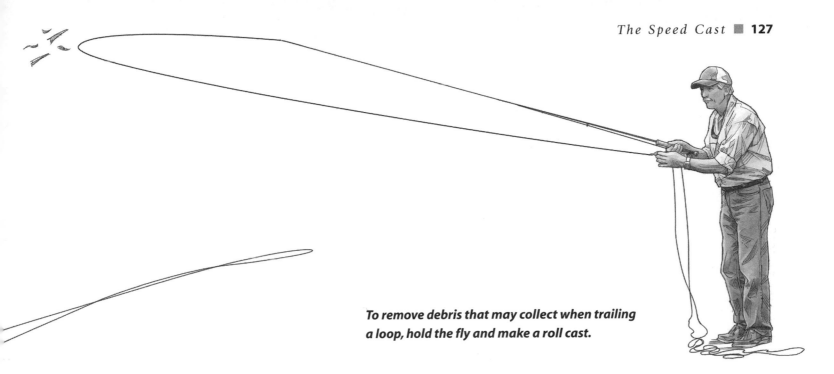

To remove debris that may collect when trailing a loop, hold the fly and make a roll cast.

most easily accomplished by stripping in line while false-casting until the length has been reduced enough for the presentation.

As a result of becoming anxious or at the behest of a guide or friend to hurry, some fly fishers futilely try to hasten the delivery without allowing enough time for the rod to load at the completion of each false cast. But the fundamentals of speed casts are the same as with all casts, and any attempts to shortcut these basics by rushing will certainly botch the presentation. Therefore, developing a sound and fast delivery is critical for consistent success in the most time-demanding situations.

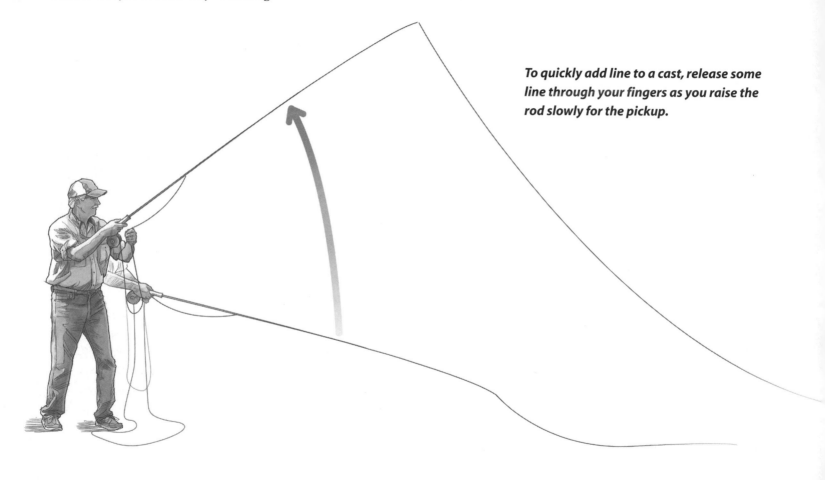

To quickly add line to a cast, release some line through your fingers as you raise the rod slowly for the pickup.

To quickly decrease the length of line for a short cast, strip in line while false-casting.

Fly casting executed to perfection is a blend of art, athleticism, and physics—fly, leader, line, rod, and angler moving as a synchronized unit. If you're willing to consistently practice the techniques in this book, you can achieve that level of casting performance and your enjoyment on the water will increase significantly as a result. I hope that *Performance Fly Casting* becomes a frequent reference and continues to play a principal role in improving your fly-fishing skills for years to come.

index